Pi of Life

Hi Demi,

Thank YOU for coordinating all the logistics for the parent workshops today! Having parents at both the morning & afternoon sessions helped with the day's success!! I hope the words in this book speak to the energy and thoughtfulness that you put in to help make this memorable day 😊

Cheers,
Sunil

MAR 11/2019

Praise for Pi of Life

"With his heart on his sleeve and his love for both life and mathematics undeniably proclaimed, Sunil Singh has written a wonderful—if too brief—introduction to why and how mathematics can be a source of joy. Too few people see mathematics as a study of the connective tissues in life. This book places that idea front and center. It will be required reading in my future undergraduate mathematics courses."— **Christopher S. Brownell, PhD,** Program Director, Mathematics and STEM Education Programs, Fresno Pacific University; Senior Mathematics Education Researcher at the AIMS Center for Math and Science Education

"Sunil is a meta-mathematical popularizer with a distinctly original voice who has responded to the zeitgeist surrounding Mathematics with a courageous, hopeful, challenging, invitational, and loving gift for *all* ages. Deftly navigating the worlds of mathematical history, mythology, and 'discovery,' the narrative weaves these together with a diverse and eclectic mix of inter-generational popular culture references, anecdote, and autobiography that is a testament to what it means to fall in love with doing Mathematics. By juxtaposing some of the most powerful human ideas and stories with some of the most powerful human emotions, *Pi of Life: The Hidden Happiness of Mathematics*, creates an opportunity for nurturing networks of more positive, joyful associations with mathematics. A transformative encounter awaits no matter what your past or current relationship status with Mathematics. 'Three point one four/this is a math book you must explore!'"—**Dr. Steven Khan**, Popularizations of Mathematics Researcher, Assistant Professor Program Coordinator, Technological Education, Brock University

"*Pi of Life* is a masterful work that grips the reader, whether he be a lover or hater of mathematics, by exposing the intricately woven web between mathematics and humanity itself. Sunil has put into words the true answer to the age-old question 'when are we going to use this in real life?' As you read his chapters, the desire to ask that question will crumble away and you'll turn back to the world around you and the existence you live with newly opened eyes. Sunil's experiences will resonate with your own as they did mine. As a teacher, *Pi of Life* reminded me of the mathematical empathy I need to have for my students as they learn new ideas for the first time. Read this book with an open mind toward mathematics, and when you've finished it you'll have a newfound courage to embrace a Real Life."—**Denis Sheeran**, Mathematics Professor, K–12 Educator and author of *Instant Relevance: Using Today's Experiences to Teach Tomorrow's Lessons*

"*Pi of Life* elegantly integrates ideas found in pure mathematics, mathematics history, and discovery with ideas about teaching and learning mathematics. Singh gently challenges all of us to rethink our own ideas and beliefs while providing bridges between formal and informal mathematics. The reader will feel connected through the author's clever sense of metaphor and his use of stories that reveal the ordinary person's math experiences. I highly recommend this read for those who are looking for reason and connections between school mathematics and the mathematics of mathematicians!"—**Dr. Debbie Plowman**, Coordinator for Mathematics Initiative, University of Texas

"*Pi of Life* helps us to truly appreciate the joy, the peace, and the beauty of mathematics. Sunil Singh's perceptive understanding of the link between mathematics and all aspects of life, allows us to see, without question, how mathematics connects everyone to everything. Such a powerful read and forever indebted by these new connections!"—**Laurie Bloomfield**, author of *Finding Felicia* and *The Everything Parent's Guide to Common Core Science Grades 6–8: Understand the New Science Standards to Help Your Child Learn and Succeed*

"Sunil Singh demonstrates how mathematics is a human endeavor filled with stories of struggle and hope, and makes a passionate plea for educators to adopt a 'Slow Math' movement: to teach fewer topics deeper, to focus on questions rather than answers, to present challenging problems to develop resistance and resilience in our students, and above all, to emphasize the joy and happiness of creating mathematics. Through eleven chapters (appropriately given titles such as 'gratitude,' 'simplicity,' and 'connection'), Singh shows how students can taste the delicious offerings of mathematics rather than the 'processed staples' of our present-day curriculum, through an in-depth exploration of fractals, prime numbers, Sudoku puzzles, and logic puzzles. The chapter on Mathematical Expectation, and the discussion of how casinos and insurance companies take advantage of mathematical illiteracy, is particularly insightful. *Pi of Life* is Singh's love letter to mathematics, where he reveals how the pursuit of mathematics leads to our happiness."—**Richard Hoshino**, Math Professor, Quest University Canada, and author of *The Math Olympian*

"*Pi of Life* is Sunil Singh's way of showing that mathematics is happiness. Hard to believe? Not after you read this book! Sunil demonstrates with conviction that, because math is deep in all our lives, everyone should be able to appreciate it. And like happiness, 'math will find you'!"—**Renée Michaud**, Coordinator of Mathematics, Consortium Provincial Francophone Alberta

Pi of Life

The Hidden Happiness of Mathematics

Sunil Singh

ROWMAN & LITTLEFIELD
Lanham • Boulder • New York • London

Published by Rowman & Littlefield
A wholly owned subsidiary of
The Rowman & Littlefield Publishing Group, Inc.
4501 Forbes Boulevard, Suite 200, Lanham, Maryland 20706
www.rowman.com

Unit A, Whitacre Mews, 26-34 Stannary Street, London SE11 4AB

British Library Cataloguing in Publication Information Available

Library of Congress Cataloging-in-Publication Data

Names: Singh, Sunil (Mathematics teacher)
Title: Pi of life : hidden happiness of mathematics / Sunil Singh.
Description: Lanham : Rowman & Littlefield, [2017] | Includes index.
Identifiers: LCCN 2017014528 (print) | LCCN 2017019061 (ebook) | ISBN
    9781475833775 (Electronic) | ISBN 9781475833751 (cloth : alk. paper) |
    ISBN 9781475833768 (pbk. : alk. paper)
Subjects: LCSH: Mathematics—Miscellanea.
Classification: LCC QA99 (ebook) | LCC QA99 .S4825 2017 (print) | DDC
    510—dc23
LC record available at https://lccn.loc.gov/2017014528

∞™ The paper used in this publication meets the minimum requirements
of American National Standard for Information Sciences—Permanence of
Paper for Printed Library Materials, ANSI/NISO Z39.48-1992.

Printed in the United States of America

For Papa, Mummy, Aidan, and Raya

Contents

Foreword

What is mathematics?

Math is humility, simplicity, courage, curiosity, gratitude, health, power, resilience, laughter, connection, and hope. Math is that which speaks to human truth and soulful joy, and yet transcends our humanness. It is the paradox of creativity and utility united. It is the surprise of discovering something you felt you somehow knew all along, but didn't. To stare into math is to stare into the cosmos, to experience visceral alarm and ebullient joy hand in hand, to see one's own insignificance and yet find meaning simply from being. Mathematics is the portal to the playground of the soul.

As a child, I liked to contemplate mathematics.

I was an intensely shy young lad and led a very lonely internal childhood. I contemplated all sorts of "big questions" in a search for significance, meaning, and connection. And there was one thought experience that brought me directly to mathematics. It came from asking a question no doubt asked by 10-year-olds galore, generation after generation.

Aliens. If they are out there, how could we communicate with them? What is a universal experience we share and can talk about from afar?

My answer back then was not at all original to the world (thank you, Carl Sagan). But my thought process, logical gaps and all, was nonetheless original to me.

Communication: What is that? It is an interaction between two entities. As such, each entity must be aware that there are two entities.

If this is not the case—that is, if one of the beings has no sense of "self" and "other," then we have no hope of communicating. The issue of trying to do so is then moot. (So let's forget about trying to talk to intelligent clouds of amorphous gas.)

We are reduced, then, to the situation of trying to communicate with a being equally aware of the existence of two states. So we should make use of two distinct symbols, like 0 and 1, in our communication efforts and explore the idea of counting, counting discrete things. Okay. Binary arithmetic comes to mind. And we should use it to communicate numbers.

Now, which numbers seem to be universal and interesting and are likely to grab an alien's attention?

It has to be the prime numbers.

I decided, from this argument, that mathematics was my way to connect with the universe.

And then there was my schooling.

My primary school and high school experiences of mathematics seemed intent to convince me of the opposite, that mathematics was disconnected from universal meaning. I was caught in the 1970s Australian Anglophilic model of mathematics instruction—just memorize and do—and, being a compliant (and did I mention shy?) child, I complied. It was, by and large, a joyless time in my mathematical experience.

I did once challenge the system by asking a question in class. (Frustration got the best of me.) In a unit on the Pythagorean Theorem, our teacher had each student draw three examples of right triangles, measure their side lengths, and observe that "a squared plus b squared equals c squared" each and every time. There were 37 students in the room, with me one of them. I asked: "Excuse me, Sir. How do we know that it wasn't just coincidence that this happened to work 111 times in a row?" (Never mind I was fully aware that, with measurement error, no one actually saw the result as true in the first place. I let that issue slide.) The response I received for my outspokenness was curt. "Go back and draw another three triangles."

This knockback may have been a brilliant pedagogical ploy, as it did spur me on to try to figure out or find out by myself how to justify the Pythagorean Theorem. (I do remember later coming across the striking visual proof of the result of arranging four copies of the same right triangle in a big square two different ways. But without algebra, or at least numbers, anywhere on the page I concluded that this visual beauty probably wouldn't be allowed in a math class.)

But the knockback, of course, had another potent consequence: it reinforced my conclusion that universal thinking was outside the societal definition of what math was and thus should be kept a private enterprise. In other words, quite simply, I was not doing actual math. *Why* and *what if* questions belonged outside of the classroom. Only computational *what* questions could be entertained within school walls.

I behaved and completed all those *what* questions with demonstrable fluency. I was labeled as exceptionally good at math. But I was thoroughly bored by it all. Thank goodness I was compelled to continue entertaining "non-math" ideas in my private world. A five-by-five grid of squares imprinted on a bedroom ceiling was my mathematical savior for those years.

I grew up in an old Victorian house with a patterned pressed-tin ceiling in each room of the house. My bedroom ceiling had a simple geometric set of lines forming a symmetric set of 25 squares. And each and every night throughout my childhood I fell asleep staring at that grid. Of course, I made up puzzles for myself based on that five-by-five array.

First my questions too were computational: *How many different squares could I see?* (55.) *How many rectangles could I count?* (225.) And so on. But matters soon morphed into deeper realms. *Why is the count of squares of a particular size always a square number?* (For example, there are 16 two-by-two squares in the grid, and 9 three-by-three squares.) *What is an efficient way to count rectangles? And is the fact that 225 is also a square number significant?*

Then the grid became a source of pure magical play. For example, looking at the cells along the diagonals of the grid magically reveals the sum $1 + 2 + 3 + 4 + 5 + 4 + 3 + 2 + 1$. And since the diagonals account for all the cells in the grid, this sum, without a lick of arithmetic, must come to 25. And then, in a flash, the realization that immense power was at hand struck hard: I can sum all the numbers from one up to a million and back down again in a split second. The answer must be one million squared. (In those days, that number was called a *billion* in the

United Kingdom and the Commonwealth.) Whoa! Try doing that sum directly on one of those new-fangled calculators!

Fast forward a few decades and we have the mathematics education system of today. It is so much more joyous and freeing and buoyant from that of my day. We are starting to give space to discuss—even discover—structure, to play with pattern, to see answers as invitations to ask more, and to offer *why*, *what else*, and maybe even *what if* questions welcome within the curriculum walls.

Starting.

It is a slow turn of the education tanker, maybe just a fraction of a degree, but it is a turn. Nothing from the past has been sacrificed—the fear of the parental body, it seems—as we develop context, story, and relevance in the curriculum experience. Computation and doing sits hand in hand with thinking and expanding ideas. The student experience of mathematics is becoming human. (And before we know it, large five-by-five grids of squares might be painted on every classroom ceiling!)

And then there is the education visionary, Sunil Singh, pushing the mathematics experience for students and guides alike to glorious cosmic heights. From seeing diagonal and gnomon patterns in square stacks of building blocks with elementary school children and discovering perfect numbers along the way, to playing with deep mathematical structures with parents, to linking parabolas to make smooth roller coaster rides with high school students, Sunil brings the creative force of mathematical wonder to the fore. He opens eyes to the awe of mathematics.

I first met this kindred spirit through e-mail, as a fellow from Ontario starting a new innovative school and mathematics playground, the Right Angle, just wanting to reach out and let me know of the dream he was pursuing. His passion for mathematics and for sharing joyous mathematics was apparent from the get-go—it oozed from between the lines on the screen—and he had my full support right away. I recognized something special, a force that was strong, one that was not going to be squelched by the twists and turns of life (and there were some). In fact, the fates of life only strengthened Sunil's love for mathematics, and here we are today, with this book, a testimony of the human power of mathematics.

The world is ready for a global love affair with mathematics. The time is right. And Sunil has written the love letter of our time.

Humility, simplicity, courage, curiosity, gratitude, health, power, resilience, laughter, connection, and hope. These human conditions sum up the true mathematical experience. They define the mathematics of the soul. They link our individualities with the cosmos and thereby link each of our selves with each other. Mathematics is the portal to awe—true human, cosmic awe.

Mathematics itself is inescapable. To prove it, choose any appearance of one of the words *humility, simplicity, courage, curiosity, gratitude, health, power, resilience, laughter, connection,* or *hope* in this foreword, count how many letters are in that word. Then count that many words forward in this text. For example, starting with the first appearance of *humility* in this very paragraph we count forward eight places to *laughter,* also of eight letters, which then takes us to *how* with three letters, which then takes us to *are,* and then *word,* and so on. Count this way through the entire foreword and find they each lead to this word: *MATH*!

This book speaks to the mathematical heart: my mathematical heart, your mathematical heart. It puts into words the natural childhood love of the subject and sets that love free. It is an expression of the ineluctable exuberance of true mathematics. The *Pi of Life,* with its tangible pieces (a circumference and a diameter), its infinitude (a non-repeating decimal), and its transcendence (a transcendental number) is a true celebration of life. Welcome, mathematics. Welcome back home.

Dr. James Tanton
Ambassador, Mathematical Association of America
Founder of The Global Math Project

Introduction

We are born to be happy. Childhood, for the obvious reasons of endless play and laughter, will always be our most natural vessel for happiness. It is a gift. We get it for free. But, in some cruel twist of fate, the conclusion of childhood marks the onset of the most unnecessary journeys in so many lives.

This would be the slow death march through education's desert—mathematics. Thirsting for relevance, context, and meaning, so many of us have wandered aimlessly—with nary a sense of hope or belief in a worthy destination or purpose. The clear majority of us, regardless of how or why we survived in this parched environment, have been reporting back to society—for decades now—that we never found that promised oasis. We just gulped down school's castor oil and believed its dispenser's message: *you need it; it's important in life.*

The confirmation of these tortuous metaphors is littered all over social media. Just search Twitter and Facebook for "Math Sucks" or "I Hate Math" and you will find communities in the thousands exacting revenge through tweets, posts, and memes. Unfortunately, all of this is the result of a light take on Newton's Third Law: *for every action, there is an equal and opposite reaction.* In this case, all the frustration, anxiety, confusion, and boredom that classroom mathematics caused millions of students is being volleyed back with a disdain that is not only real—it is *valid.* But, this was not only completely avoidable, it went against the very nature of our being. You see, we were *also* born to love mathematics.

The fact that a sizable population drifted into a hardened contempt for what is basically a human endeavor is not just an oversight or an error to be cataloged in the banal files of "Some People Are Not Good at Math." It is a tragedy. In *King Lear*, the titular character disinherits Cordelia, the daughter he *should* have loved the most. In education, students banish mathematics with the same hostility. Yet, unlike Shakespeare's classic play, there is no reconciliation or amends at the end. *Mathematics* was sadly written to be anticlimactic and unresolved. If this were truly the theater, the production of *Mathematics* would have been shut down after the first performance. Its confusing and disconnected narrative, directed by education, would not have lasted—as it has—for over 100 years.

In 2012, Deepak Malhotra, professor at the Harvard Business School, gave a luminary speech to the graduating MBA class of that same year. The talk was titled "Tragedy and Genius." It has now over 400,000 views on YouTube. It is a 45-minute presentation that frames its contemplative theme in just a few minutes.

> Tragedy is the gulf between how happy you should have been and how happy you actually are. Genius is closing that delta.
>
> —Deepak Malhotra, Harvard Business School

Mathematics has suffered a similar fate. The gulf between how happy mathematics should have made most of us and how unhappy it currently makes us is a gap that is yawning beyond anything you could ever imagine. Compounding matters is that the beauty of mathematics is often heavily cloaked in poorly explained formulas or just flat-out ignored—number theory and geometry are embedded everywhere in nature!

> Joy in looking and comprehending is nature's most beautiful gift.
>
> —Albert Einstein

Looking at the chalkboard in class would have been valuable if you also would have looked out the window—to see trees, flowers, and grass, dancing and breathing mathematics. Math is bursting with color and poetry, and our mission should be to collectively decode it in a way that warms the heart *first* and *then* interacts with our brain. If your knowledge of mathematics ever eclipses your love for it, then both will be doomed. Mathematics is a code for the universe created by humans. That alone should be prompting the joy and curiosity that Einstein suggested. But it doesn't. There are other barriers.

You don't have to have a lick of musical talent to completely appreciate the brilliance of a concert pianist. You just need to hear. Your brain will translate the audible mathematics to release dopamine, the signal that you are appreciating and understanding what you are hearing. You could have had trouble with even a basic Paint-By-Numbers kit, but still get completely lost in a longing gaze at a painting by a great artist. The visual mathematics of lines and proportion will often yield pleasing responses. Often, the more complex the mathematics in a piece of art, the more visually drawn we will be to that image.

Is your cooking so horrible that you can't even make toast? Doesn't matter. You don't have to be a gourmet chef to slump in your seat like a satisfied Anthony Bourdain after eating at Thomas Keller's French Laundry in Napa Valley. So much of this beautiful world can be seen, read, heard, and tasted. While we may not be able to reach such creative heights, we will always have the senses and sensibilities to value the artist and their craft. The admiration and understanding will never have impedance. The artistic currency will never suffer any devaluation. There will be no exhaustive and costly debates as to what value is added to our lives by these basic expressions of human potential.

This is not the case for mathematics. Never has been. Primarily because it has never been looked upon as an *art form* by society—more like cerebral ditch digging, to implement and explain practical matters to those who would be interested in such drudgery. Despite it having brilliant *writers*, *painters*, and *composers*, and having a 20,000-year-old story that is filled with heroism, endurance, pleasure, and pain, the lasting verdict by society is that it seems to be a necessary . . . *evil*.

Without mathematics, it would not be an exaggeration to say it would be Dickensian squalor meets *The Flintstones*. No computers. No medical devices. No telescopes. No televisions. No cell phones. That's for starters. But that's not why we should be interested in mathematics, the humble servant of advancing societies.

No. Our collective interest should be in seeing mathematics reflected, refracted, and illuminated through a softer, more human, historical lens—appealing to our heart. Having emotional connections to its patterning and symmetry that are so deep that it can contribute to our spirit for life is where the bar must be set. To merely convey it as some disconnected heap of information with practicality that is trivial or exaggerated to baffle our brains is low-hanging fruit—which *still* goes unpicked by so many of us.

> Mathematics is one of the essential emanations of the human spirit,
> a thing to be valued in and for itself, like art or poetry.
>
> —Oscar Veblen

Rewinding back to Malhotra's speech, when he introduced the title of his talk to a packed audience of people with the highest potential for wealth, health, and social standing in the entire world, he also issued a statistical warning. He said that many of the people in the audience, despite having the top 1/100th of 1 percent potential for all those measures of success, will be *unhappy* at some point in their lives. This is proof that happiness is not a function of luck, hard work, or external acquisition. It is an internal occupation, as is passionately communicated in Sylvia Boorstein's book, *Happiness Is an Inside Job*.

The beauty of mathematics lies in this internal occupation of trying to see its permanence (ideas that will last forever). Gorgeous ideas drawn up with the same aesthetic of any masterpiece found in art, literature, and music. But, before we can even break down the mathematics to view it in such a glowing light, we need to break down deeper elements of our lives—the universal characteristics of happiness.

In February 2017, *Quanta Magazine* did an interview with Francis Su, mathematician at the prestigious Harvey Mudd College in California. The core ideas of the article revolved around an emotional talk that Su gave as outgoing president of the Mathematical Association of America. That talk was called "Mathematics for Human Flourishing." In that speech—which left many in the audience in tears—Su spoke of living a life filled with beauty, truth, justice, play, and love. All of which are found in mathematics.

This book is about going on that journey and finding eleven key elements that yield the life that Su passionately alludes to—a life lived well—which, in the end, means a happy life. So, each chapter has a simple—but mysterious—mathematical title and is accompanied by an italicized theme that is rooted in a familiar virtue for living well—living happily.

As such, this book is not only about giving you a more human insight into the universe's most elegant and important language. It is also about discussing it in ways that reflect the cadence of our own communication—little conversations, joyful storytelling, and pleasant diversions. It is in this network of honest conversations where the pillars of our happiness live—the thankfully non-quantifiable virtues and aspirations of being human.

And nestled comfortably in these universal markers for being happy are rich mathematical ideas. Society has been teaching us math for the longest time. It's time to flip that lens and examine what math can teach *society*—beyond facts, figures, and applications. It can reflect values and traits that we, as a society, cherish and strive to hold.

The style of writing in this book was purposefully crafted to make *math* a verb; to make it blissfully animated—to make it sing, dance, laugh, and cry. To make it as bloody real and raw as possible. It is my intention that every part of this book comes off as how I would talk about mathematics in settings that are part of our social and recreational vernacular—at a noisy bar on a Thursday night, around a campfire past midnight, or on a bus talking to a stranger. Even the images in the book are the same goofy and disarming doodles I might try to scrawl on a slightly beer-soaked restaurant napkin!

The story of mathematics is a most compelling yarn. If only I could sit with you on a breezy porch with a glass of wine in hand and confess it all, thinking that we have all the time in the world—when we do not. It's that internal tension of trying to share *every* meaningful morsel of math, but in a leisurely and satisfying fashion, that drove me to write this book. It's akin to drinking a great red—slowly, purposefully, and reflectively. In the 2004 movie *Sideways*, Miles (Paul Giamatti) is transfixed by the thoughts of Maya (Virginia Madsen) on the life of wine. Sitting on a porch in the Californian night sky, the most romantic elements of wine and honesty are uncorked.

I want to tell you about the life of mathematics and hopefully cast a spell of new emotions and ideas. Math's splendor is vast. You will never know how vast. Neither will I. Perhaps it's a bit melancholic (or perhaps it's the wine talking), but I believe the beauty of life lies in the surplus of questions and deficit of time.

> Life's splendor forever lies in wait about each one of us in all its fullness, but veiled from view, deep down, invisible, far off. It is there, though, not hostile, not reluctant, not deaf. If you summon it by the right word, by its right name, it will come.
>
> —Franz Kafka

It's time to go deep within ourselves with mathematics as our gentle guide and discover what has always truly been mathematics' most important contribution to us—happiness. In our sometimes-exhausting search for joy and meaning in life, we somehow neglected to examine the softer yolk inside math's shell. That beauty and joy of life have *always* been available. The happiness of mathematics awaits you . . .

CHAPTER 1

Zero

Humility

The only wisdom is the knowledge that you know nothing.

—Socrates

One Friday in April, some students in a Canadian college class decided to have a lunch that was more liquid than solid—specifically, a beer to nachos ratio that easily eclipsed 2 to 1. Punctuality for the afternoon math class fell low on the priority list for many of the students and, for that matter, the teacher as well. Professor Dave Alexander, a highly respected math professor at the Faculty of Education in Toronto, was a very wise, understanding, and outgoing soul. His approach to teaching mirrored the general disdain for structure found in many of his students. The teacher was no ordinary teacher, and I was merely one of his admiring students.

It is April 1992. I am at Teacher's College at the University of Toronto. While our class contained some brilliant students, it also created and housed a lot of pranksters and provocateurs. We were the general antithesis of the graduating class of future teachers. Our presentations, while rooted in academic research, tended to be framed by undetected mockery of the institutional and factory feel of teacher education. "Teaching is more art than science" would be the guiding mantra of our collective rebellion.

On this day—our last math education class before exams—our well-meaning defiance was spiked with the hoppy and fruity notes of our favorite draft beer. Dave was unsurprisingly indifferent to our late and laughing entrance. In fact, I distinctly remember him staring out the window in some quasi-Kafka fashion as we found our seats. Most days this could have meant nothing. Not today. He had sort of a mischievous glow—hinting at putting us disenfranchised know-it-alls finally in our place. (Spoiler alert: he did!)

He asked us to discuss in our table groups the most important qualities of being a great teacher. Once we had compiled our list as a group, we would share the results with the rest of the class. Even though the dwindling hours of Friday classes and mild happiness of drinking a few pints in a blistering sun were influencing our interest level, the question posed by Dave had us all collaborating rather quickly.

This was, after all, our chance to punctuate our teacher education with our belief that teaching was indeed an art form of the highest calling. Every group was finished within fifteen to twenty minutes. The energy and volume level of the class suggested that every group was confident that they had written the "Ten Commandments of Teaching."

The first group went up. I cannot recall their answers, but I am sure they put "knowledge" in their list. After they were done, Dave simply said, "Thank you. Next." What? No affirming "good job"? No gold stars? Where was the feedback? To make matters more confusing, Dave kept looking out the window quite a bit during the rest of the presentations. His posture and gaze were more philosophical than scholarly. He could have easily replaced his casual jacket with a toga that afternoon.

Even when our group offered "humor" as an important criterion for successful teaching, he was unmoved by our choice. The window seemed to offer more interest than responses to a crucial question from future teachers. What was going on? We would come to learn that Dave was not so much disinterested in our answers, he was only confident that no group would come up with the two responses he had in mind. Just two . . .

Yes. Despite giving us a red herring requirement that was arguably unbounded, there were only two qualities that Dave felt were needed for a lifelong career of happy and successful teaching: honesty and being a mutual learner. Even as Dave started to explain his philosophical simplicity, I soon felt his voice recede into this muddied tone that you might hear in a movie or TV show—signaling some pivotal moment of reflection for the protagonist. It was something right out of *The Wonder*

Years! Teaching was not so much an art form; it was simply about be-ing . . . human.

The week prior, we were sitting in this same class examining how to effectively model mathematics for students. Symbols and formulas were discussed with proper pedagogical language. There was plenty of resonance with our brains. Today, our last day, was all about the heart. So, while Dave had given some outstanding strategies for teaching mathematics with engagement and clarity the entire year, he wanted our lasting impression of everything—him, our class, teaching, and such—ending in the often-overlooked simplicity of our own humanity.

Mathematics should be taught as a human endeavor filled with sto-ries of hope, struggle, pleasure, courage, and such. This statement is a partial treasure map for finding math gold. It is far from being a clear or complete map. It is simply subtle instructions to shift the rudder on the novice boat of teaching. To try and veer away from the soon-to-be-familiar waters of formula memorization, procedural memorization, and problem memorization.

These waters are more like whirlpools where we expend valuable energy in just not going . . . *under*. Avoiding drowning, while fatiguing, is a necessary struggle to not only make sense of the purest purpose of mathematics, but just to make sense of it *all*. Period.

THE BIRTH OF NOTHING

Zero. Zilch. Zip. Nil. Naught. They all generally mean the same thing—nothing. India, which gave the world the universal counting system we know today, also gave us zero. A five-hour train ride south of New Delhi will bring you to the city of Gwalior, one of many cities in India that is overseen by an impressive fort. If you take the path upward toward the fort, you will approach a tiny temple. It is here that the pil-grimage of many mathematicians ends: a small, 100-square-foot room that requires most people to duck their heads slightly upon entering.

On one of the walls is an inscription that dates to the late ninth century. It is filled with numbers. And, nestled among these familiar numbers of one to nine is the *new* number—zero. It occurs twice on the wall. One instance is in the number 50, with the familiar circle to represent zero. The number here represents the daily gift of 50 garlands of flowers. It is fitting that the earliest recording of this revolutionary number would be attached to the colorful beauty of nature. (Those interested in learning more should read the marvelous *Zero: The Biography of a Dangerous Idea* by Charles Siefe.)

India made another valuable contribution to the world, almost parallel in nature. This would be the idea of *nirvana*, the transcendent state of "nothingness," when you are liberated from suffering and desires. In fact, the word used in philosophical texts to mean nothing, or the void, is *shunya*, the same word later used to mean zero. A number that literally means "nothing" is the spiritual anchor for one of the world's oldest civilizations. *Shunya* means a sort of salvation—by emptying ourselves.

According to Renu Jain, professor of mathematics at Jiwaji University in Gwalior, "When all our desires are nullified, then we go to nirvana or *shunya* or total salvation." In the modern world, it is common to see religion and science as always in conflict. Yet in ancient India, mathematics and spirituality are forever intertwined.

George Gheverghese Joseph, author of *The Crest of the Peacock: Non-European Roots of Mathematics*, and one of the leading math historians in the world, reinforces this milestone birth and reason for zero. That it happened when an unknown Indian mathematician, about 2,000 years ago, realized that "this philosophical and cultural concept would also be useful in a mathematical sense." Zero's practicality is a flower that grew out of the seed of pure bliss!

It is this idea of zero that frames not only this chapter, but essentially the whole book—to discover the simple kernels of truth and joy in the experience and processes involved with mathematics. And, much like the journey to the remote site in which this mathematical treasure is found, so will be the ascent to mathematical happiness—filled with broken paths, hidden trails, and secret passages. This journey *is* our destination. There is no end point. We start and just never finish. Thankfully!

But, our first step to go forward is to take a large step back. This step is necessary to see and appreciate the enormity of mathematics. We must unchain ourselves from the idea that the accumulation of knowledge with velocity is going to take us to some mathematical land of milk and honey. We need to hitch ourselves to a less impatient view of mathematics, and slow down so we can be humbled by it. The path to mathematical seduction starts here. We will never see it all. We must be in awe of this fact. Always.

Without humility, there can be no humanity.

—John Buchan

The beauty of mathematics, its intricate and often invisible tapestry that intertwines our lives, can serve as the window into appreciating the unknown, unseen, and unspoken. Mathematics has the power to explain even unremarkable ideas with remarkable elegance and grace. So much so, it is arguably the greatest reflection of our own humanity. And, its noblest achievements could not have occurred without its artists—society has still not understood this deserving title for mathematicians—demonstrating humility. Seeing the world through wider and gentler eyes is all that is required!

But before anything of philosophical value can be added by zero, it is important to wade into mathematical waters and see—for yourself—how simple and complicated zero can be! When you add or subtract zero from a number, the result is the number you started with. $12 + 0$ and $12 - 0$ both give you 12. You might be thinking—*that was obvious. Obvious* might be the most dangerous word used in teaching and learning mathematics. It can not only create an unhealthy haste in learning math, but it can also truncate potentially rich discussions.

Zero is a concept that is ripe with contemplative questions. A situation that causes one of the most trouble is when we should divide a number by . . . gulp . . . zero! If there is one operation that has left the strongest residue of discomfort with math, it must be division. And this is because division led us all into that dangerous lair of *fractions*—the first *f word* we learned. Part of the problem is that division divorced us from our comfort zone of just adding numbers.

Math was perfectly fine when we restricted our learning to summing up stuff. Even multiplication seemed understandable—it was just the Ferrari of adding. Instead of adding up, let's say, the number 4 eight times like $4 + 4 + 4 + 4 + 4 + 4 + 4 + 4$, we might be tempted to say 4×8. But, that would be going into a bee's nest of misconception. Repeated addition is not multiplication. Repeated addition is just repeated addition. Keith Dev-lin wrote a fascinating article on this in 2008 called "It Ain't No Repeated Addition." Here we're just installing some metaphorical safety fences in our discussion, just so we don't fall downs cliffs of common misunder-standing—examining zero is challenging enough!

If you buy that subtraction is just negative addition, then you will be more at ease with division housing the concept of addition. For example, 12 divided by 2 is 6. Now just shift our idea of division to *subtracting until we get to . . . zero*! How many times can you subtract 2 from 12 until you get to zero? 12–2–2–2–2–2–2 = 0. Six times. What about 57 divided by 9? The answer is not as important as knowing that you will have something left over. You cannot take away 9 some whole number of times from 57.

Now what about something like 12 divided by 0? Is this even pos-sible? Is there an answer that makes sense? Well, start taking away zero. How many times can you subtract it from 12 until you get to zero? Try as you might, you will never get down to zero. Imagine you have no ax and are asked how many whacks it will take to chop down a tree. Go ahead—take a swing. Take as many as you like. That tree will be no closer to falling even after the millionth flail with your nonexistent ax. Similarly, you will be *stuck* at 12 forever when you try to divide by zero.

There is a danger of saying the answer is infinity, but it is undefined. There is an excellent explanation for this, but here is the simplest and most whimsical. If you say, for example, 12 divided by zero is infinity and 97 divided by zero is infinity, then 12 divided by zero must equal 97 divided by zero. Which means 12 must equal 97—since the zero denominators equal each other. Now that would be ridiculous!

However, in many ways, infinity is the yang to zero's yin. To clarify, infinity is not a number. It is an idea, with a "sleepy eight" as a symbol, to denote something without any limit. There are beastly large numbers like *Graham's Number*, which is so large that even if every digit was written the size of a subatomic particle and the observable universe was a sheet of paper, you still could not write down all the digits of this unimaginable number. Yet, it is still a finite number. It will come to an end. Infinity marches to its own incomprehensible and highly complex beat forever in a zone beyond a number line . . .

If your head is beginning to throb ever so slightly, you are not alone. Georg Cantor, the father of infinity, lived the major part of his later years in depression due to the hostility he faced because of his ideas about infinity from many of his contemporaries. In the BBC documentary *Dangerous Knowledge*, Cantor's path to insanity was perhaps due to what he had seen—infinity. Or, in Cantor's mind—*God*. There's some dark conjecturing in the documentary, but there is evidence that the idea of infinity consumed Cantor's mathematical life in ways that were unhealthy. He died in a sanatorium near the end of World War I. Infinity will be explored in greater detail later in this book.

This will not be the first time a tragedy of a key mathematical figure will be conveyed. Untimely deaths and sadness have been woven intentionally into this book to explore the lives of those who usually endured much scorn and ridicule. Yes, they were brilliant mathematicians, but that was only a subset of their lives. They usually had other creative talents . . . *and vices*. Their failures and failings made them real, which brings them and all of us to a singularity that is both comforting and awe-inspiring—being human.

Our imperfections and our horribly short 2.5 billion seconds on this planet (78 years is an age we should all be thankful to live up to!) set against the vast cosmos shrink us to . . . zero. For me, that fact is hardly daunting or depressing. It's almost purifying. It should inspire us to live each day with newfound wonder. To not take too much pride in accumulating knowledge, as there are still many mountains to climb.

> I begin with humility, I act with humility, I end with humility. Humility leads to clarity. Humility leads to an open mind and a forgiving heart. With an open mind and a forgiving heart, I see every person as superior to me in some way; with every person as my teacher, I grow in wisdom. As I grow in wisdom, humility becomes ever more my guide. I begin with humility, I act with humility, I end with humility.

> —Eric Greitens

THE POWER OF ZERO

Greitens, a former Navy SEAL officer and author of the book *Resilience*, mentions the word *humility* nine times in that quote. He is powerfully reminding us where he gets his source of inspiration to learn every day. The happy journey that is mathematics is dependent on such reverence of humility. Whether we are novices or experts, we should be connected by our availability for new awe and wonder. Zero is a great metaphor for that bond.

Now just think about all the uses of zero that we have in our culture. *Absolute zero*, the temperature at which, theoretically, all motion stops. Getting down to absolute zero has essentially the identical problem with getting up to the *speed of light*. Getting to the speed of light requires an infinite amount of work, while getting down to absolute zero requires extracting an infinite amount of heat. Just to make it clear, both are impossible. Doesn't this remind you of the yin-and-yang relationship of zero and infinity?

Ground Zero has a similar connotation of intensity—the point closest to the Earth's surface to a detonation. Zero generally means nothing, but the void that it creates leaves us with a powerful mathematical or philosophical extract. To "*zero in*" is a common idiomatic phrase to denote a high level of focus and accuracy. Zero is also commonplace in pop culture in movies and music. The mid-1990s alternative rock sensation, the Smashing Pumpkins, had a song called "Zero," which had lyrics hinting at a nihilistic connection between all of us, including a deity that shares our emptiness. Our own cultural vernacular reflects the mystery of zero—sometimes it is nothing, and sometimes it is everything.

My own idea of zero as applied to learning math is kind of a pureed mixture of all the definitions and ideas—seasoned heavily with the ancient wisdom of the Athenian philosopher and a key founder of Western philosophy, Socrates. I am just as interested in my ignorance of mathematics as I am in my knowledge of it; I am just as keen to discuss my misunderstandings and mistakes that I have made as I am with my correct ideas and notions.

Nowhere did I ever make that more apparent—or public—than when I gave a keynote address to 200 people back in 2007. These people were students in grades 4 to 6. I had been invited by a local school to speak at and be involved in their "Math Day." Perhaps a bit earlier in my career I would not have given the talk that I did. It would have been heavily weighted toward my knowledge of mathematics than to my *wonderful* ignorance.

One would never think of prefacing such a negative word with something so buoyant, so joyful, so . . . *happy*. Yet, the seeds of change in philosophical navigation were planted that innocuous and slightly inebriated afternoon in my last math education class 15 years earlier. In fact, even though this was my first keynote address, I didn't have a speech prepared. I had two ideas prepared that, looking back now, were a subconscious testimonial to my last math lesson ever in Teacher's College—be honest and always learn with the same passion.

The night before my speech, I was busy selecting a few songs that I would play over the loudspeaker as kids filed into the gymnasium and were seated by their teachers. I wanted to set a mood. I remember as a high school student always feeling a slight rush in my blood any time I heard the school band rehearsing for an assembly. Music is such a delightful balm. I figured I could play two songs. I had over 13,000 songs in my *iTunes* library at the time. I knew I wasn't going to be playing Frank Sinatra or Iron Maiden, but I still mulled over selections until well past midnight.

I chose "Yellow" by Coldplay and "This Is the Sea" by the Waterboys. One song reaches for the potential infinity of the cosmos and the other the poetic infinity of the sea. Even though I played each song many times the night before, hearing them in the makeshift auditorium gave me the required goose bumps I was hoping for. I wasn't nervous. I was just really, really happy. The second part of my keynote would be talking about my favorite mathematical hero—Sophie Germain.

SOPHIE GERMAIN

In many ways, the story of Sophie Germain represents so many of the stories of mathematics—perseverance and passion. Yet, sadly, they are told with such little frequency that they remain disconnected footnotes for the general population. They are saddled with being "math stories," when they should be plain and simple human stories! The continued mystification and misappropriation of mathematics in our society leaves most of the beautiful stories in math relegated to the academic sidelines.

Sophie's story began when she was a 13-year-old girl living in Paris in 1789—in the throes of the French Revolution. Because the streets were unsafe, Sophie was forced to stay inside her family's apartment. A curious child, she discovered her father's library. She stumbled upon the death of Archimedes. Archimedes had spent his life at Syracuse studying mathematics in relative tranquility, but when he was in his late 70s, the peace was shattered by the invading Roman army. Legend has it that during the invasion Archimedes was so engrossed in the study of a geometric figure in the sand, that he failed to respond to the questioning of a Roman soldier. Thus, he was speared to death.

Germain concluded that if somebody could be so consumed by a geometric problem that it could lead to their death, then mathematics must be the most captivating subject in the world. She was moved by this story and decided that she too must become a mathematician. Sophie pursued her studies, teaching herself Latin and Greek. She read Newton and Euler at night while wrapped in blankets as her parents slept—they had taken away her fire, her light, and her clothes to force her away from her books. Eventually her parents lessened their opposition to her studies.

As she grew up, she had to, in stealth-like fashion, obtain lecture notes from the local university. And, she even took on a nom de plume of *Monsieur Le Blanc* to hide her female identity. This would be the name she used on all her correspondence with the university. Sophie's work would eventually get recognized by what many consider the greatest mathematician ever—Carl Friedrich Gauss. Unfortunately, not only would her stellar, self-taught mathematics be recognized, so would her real gender.

To illustrate how the history of mathematics is inextricably tied to general history, Sophie Germain would not have ever corresponded with Gauss had it not been for the fact that Napoleon was invading Germany, and Gauss's life was in jeopardy—much like Archimedes. Sophie, having connections to the French army, asked that his life be spared. Sophie would write a letter profusely apologizing for her deceit to Gauss. Gauss would, in return, write back one of the greatest letters ever written—smashing the stereotypes of the day to smithereens. The following excerpt from that letter was wonderfully woven in Simon Singh's international bestseller *Fermat's Enigma*.

But how to describe to you my admiration and astonishment at seeing my esteemed correspondent Monsieur Le Blanc metamorphose himself into this illustrious personage who gives such a brilliant example of what I would find it difficult to believe. A taste for the abstract sciences in general and above all the mysteries of numbers is excessively rare: one is not astonished at it: the enchanting charms of this sublime science reveal only to those who have the courage to go deeply into it. But when a person of the sex which, according to our customs and prejudices, must encounter infinitely more difficulties than men to familiarize herself with these thorny researches, succeeds nevertheless in surmounting these obstacles and penetrating the most obscure parts of them, then without doubt she must have the noblest courage, quite extraordinary talents and superior genius.

Of course, this is an abridged and age-appropriate version of this story. Sophie was one of the greatest mathematicians and fighters of all time. Her story should be inside every math textbook. It is a source of inspiration for not only students, but teachers as well. It is clear now that this story would catch your attention, but 15 minutes ago, we needed to talk about the *storyteller* before the story. Readers should really know the truth about Sunil Singh and mathematics.

At the start of the 2007 keynote address I described earlier in this chapter, one of the teachers introduced me; some polite applause followed, along with some adorable howling. I took the mic, thanked the school for inviting me, and tried to make meaningful eye contact with some of the students as I spoke. After just a minute or so, I turned to my right and started walking away from the center of the floor. I went right to the wall and turned around with my back firmly pressed against it. Before I started speaking, I could tell this physical change in speaking location was surprising many kids and teachers in the audience.

"See that wall on the other side?" I asked in a commanding, but soothing voice. "That wall represents all the mathematical knowledge in the universe. The wall that I am standing against represents just knowing that $1 + 1 = 2$. I am going to start walking toward that wall. I want people to start yelling "stop" when I am where they think I should be—how much math do you think Mr. Singh knows?"

The instructions were clear and the anticipation high. I started walking. Besides a few murmurs, natural giggling, and talking, there wasn't any indication from the supportive audience to halt my walk. After all, I was supposed to be this mathematical superhero, someone who knows libraries upon libraries of mathematical knowledge. I got halfway across the gym floor, and I heard a few "stops," but nothing largely collective for me to do so.

However, I did slow the pace of my gait. And somewhere about 75 percent of the length of the floor, I heard enough of these instructive stops to end my journey across this figurative floor of mathematical smarts. I turned around and squarely faced the audience, slightly tilting my head back to the right to compensate for my off-center location. I shook my head. "Sorry, this is not where I am supposed to be," I said with contrived lament. I rotated my body to the right, strongly indicating I would be heading back in the opposite direction. While there was some deflation of enthusiasm in the audience that I would not be this omniscient being of numbers, there was marked curiosity as to where Mr. Singh would end up.

I repeated the instructions, and this time there was an overwhelming response to stop in the middle of the gym floor. This is where I started the presentation, and perhaps it made compromising sense for me to end up there again. I did take a quick glance over my left shoulder as I *passed* this logical halfway point. Many kids were wearing faces of mild shock to confusion. "Who the heck is this mathematical impostor!" was probably a common thought.

I shuffled my feet to exaggerate the notion I was perhaps shameful of where I was going to end up—which was the wall where I had started. I put my back against the wall and held the piece of paper that was purposefully in my hands the whole time. I bent down and put the paper between the heels of my shoes and the *one plus one* wall. "This is how much mathematics I know," I trumpeted with what was surely confusing enthusiasm. I said some more words, but the expressions on the kids' faces—and the teachers—alerted me that I had made my point passionately clear. *All of us, more or less, are at the beginning of mathematical understanding.*

And the beginning is where we will always be—this large huddle of eager learners should not be afraid to ask questions, show confusion, make mistakes, stumble, and fall. We will help each other—always—since mathematics teaches us that simply being human and vulnerable teaches that even more.

BRINGING ZERO INTO OUR CLASSROOMS

Every day we should wish a question or an idea would come to the surface where we will have the grateful opportunity to proudly proclaim our minuscule knowledge of mathematics. It seems exhausting that every day in math classes all around the world there is unreasonable focus on the *knowing*. As hinted at in the keynote in 2007, even a math teacher might possess 0.1 percent of the mathematical knowledge in the universe—*hopefully*, even less!

For teachers to spend every minute of their teaching life dancing on the head of a pin would be disheartening and disingenuous. Kids should want to know the problems their teachers never solved, and the ideas that are *still* unclear to them to this day.

A few years back a prominent mathematical magazine in Ontario called the *Gazette* published an article authored by a local *leader* in mathematics education. The crux of the article was a public confession to the writer's lack of understanding of a high school topic called *proof by induction*. While he had done these proofs correctly as a student and as a teacher, he admitted it was all based on parroting procedures found in books—sadly, the most central idea in how mathematics is communicated in schools.

In 2017, the popular MathTwitterBlogosophere (#MTBoS) reached out to teachers to share their moments of misunderstanding with other teachers—to lend their vulnerability to having real and honest conversations about mathematics. In essence, what was being hailed was the idea that with *collective* humility will come deeper knowledge and understanding of math for all of us.

Confusion is beyond okay. It needs a figurative seat in every classroom, to disarm and to motivate. Mathematics is not a sprint to be won. It's a marathon to simply be entered in. And, FYI, nobody finishes. For the most part, we just stand around the starting line smiling and laughing. Chris Brownell, a kindred spirit at Fresno Pacific University, sums it up all too well when teaching math to his students. "If we were a bit smarter, we wouldn't need it; a bit less intelligent we wouldn't understand it." In other words, let's relish being human. Inquisitive and humble. It's the beginning; it's also the end.

Zero. The beginning and the end. Get comfortable. It's going to be a long and strange trip. So, thank you, India. Thank you, Dave Alexander. Thanks for . . . *nothing*!

CHAPTER 2

One Plus Two

Simplicity

> Simplicity is the most difficult thing to secure in this world; it is the last limit of experience and the last effort of genius.
>
> —George Sand

Simplicity has never been more in demand in our lives. It constantly swirls around in our psyche, searching for comfort in everything from our daily routines to our pleasures, even our relationships with one another. *Blue Zones*, areas of the world that have life expectancies far greater than the average, are not the results of advanced medicines, high-profile occupations, gym memberships, or hundreds of friends. They exist due to lifestyle choices in diet, exercise, and family and that are . . . *simple.*

Quotes on simplicity not only include literary giants like Thoreau, Tolstoy, and Hemingway, but the great scientists like Boltzmann, Newton, and Einstein. Searching and finding simplicity in our universe serves a primal need for clarity and comfort. But, more than that—especially since our world has gotten increasingly distracting, noisy, and complex—harnessing simplicity is becoming less and less a luxury. Simplicity is turning out to be a life necessity.

The idea of simplicity has also given birth to two of the most successful companies—*Apple* and *Google*. Apple uses simple messages, and Google uses simple space design. Simple is in. Simple works—*always* have worked. Unfortunately, no word could be further from the truth when most people describe mathematics (which is sadly ironic because no word could be *closer* to the truth when describing mathematics).

So, where did things go wrong? Where did it go awry? Some of you might say high school. Some might cite the hormonal years of middle school. A few of us might have thrown our arms up in the air in public school, venting out our newfound cuss words about math at recess—*f#*$ fractions*! Really, our understanding of mathematics went off the rails as soon as we learned to *count to 10.* That's right. Once we had 1, 2, 3,4, 5, 6, 7, 8, 9, and 10, we should have taken a time-out—a very large time-out! Before we get to why we should have stopped to smell—heck, even *water*—the roses, let's rewind the memory tape to the experiences most of us had.

TEN: A MATHEMATICAL RED LIGHT

Once we had all become proficient at counting to 10, which usually occurs by the age of five, our parents/teachers hoisted our learning sails, and we marched on to 20, 30, 50, eventually to 100. Oh, to be able to count to *one hundred*! It's an early checkpoint for becoming familiar with counting.

> My grade 1 teacher, Mrs. Jackson, was sure to make exclamatory notes describing my milestone to 100 in my report card. I was six years old. I had 2 siblings, ate 3 meals a day, maybe owned 5 shirts and lived on the 7th floor of an apartment building. What use and meaning did I have for something like *79*? My life, for the most part, was filled with single-digit occupation and relevance.

Screaming past these numbers was not only unnecessary—it was a mistake! Teachers had all the numbers they needed to grab our interest and start cultivating a deep curiosity for mathematics. Counting and sums are only worthwhile if they lead to the heart of what a mathematician truly is*: a pattern searcher.*

If you ask a child to do 9 + 3, the answer of "12" lacks any meaningful context. Moreover, children are too often pulled out of the comfort zone of their fingers. Adding 9 + 3 with fingers necessitates nine fingers being up. As soon as the kids go past 10, both hands will form a closed fist. And, depending if they prefer the right or the left hand, two fingers will go up in one of these hands. This will be followed by a gleeful elation of "12." But, if you took a picture of this, and did not know the question, you would think two was the answer to some question. Oh my, what a temptation to teach modular math at this point!

By grade 1, we would soon get sheets with questions like $6 + 3$, $2 + 5$, $7 + 1$, etc. Unbeknownst to Mrs. Jackson, she came perilously close to letting us all fall down the rabbit hole of mathematics! If only she would have just taken the numbers 1 to 10 that we knew so well and simply inserted *plus signs* between the numbers. She might have created a class full of Germains and Gausses . . .

$$1 + 2 + 3 + 4 + 5 + 6 + 7 + 8 + 9 + 10$$

The awaiting portal—manned by *Kafka*—to the *splendor* of mathematical understanding is not in some code written in hieroglyphics or comprehension of multi-variable formulas. It lies in the fundamental idea of just adding numbers that are contained in just our hands and feet. To appreciate the rich patterning that is embedded in the above sums, it is important that we take a big step . . . *backward*.

GOING BACK AND FINDING PLAY

In the 1971 film *Willy Wonka and the Chocolate Factory*, Gene Wilder's character is responsible for some hefty literary allusions that include Shakespeare, Keats, and Wilde. Early in the film he offers typical Wonka advice to Violet Beauregarde and her father about going back: "Oh, you can't get out backwards. You must move forward to go back. Better press on." When it comes to seeing the full-color illumination of mathematics, going a Wonka slantways from counting to 10 would not only seem impractical, but *impossible*! What could possibly be mined from the numbers 1 to 10 with addition signs? At this point you might be wondering, "Where are you taking us, *Singh*?"

Let's get out of the abstract that all of us entered much too quickly. Let's go back to the time of the Incas and Mayans, and let's play with pebbles! There has always been a nagging feeling in some parts of the math community that young children can do some extraordinary mathematics in the field of *number theory*—an area that sparked the love of mathematics in, arguably, the most brilliant mathematician of all time, Carl Friedrich Gauss.

It will be of little surprise, then, to know that the mathematical link that weaves many of the subtitles of universal human traits in all the chapters will intersect this charming branch of mathematics. All play is learning, and mathematics' play begins in the sandlot of numbers. Sometimes you will be charmed by its elegance and sometimes you will be charmed by its element of surprise. But, hopefully, more than anything, you will be taken by its comforting simplicity. But, just so we are clear, mathematical simplicity is more of an elegant aesthetic to reach for. It requires patience. To have mathematical ideas be easily understood, ingenuity and clarity must partner up. So, let's turn around . . .

Most high school teachers never have an opportunity to go *backward*, to start all over again. So, when my daughter had her grade 1 teacher invite me to pay a visit to her class in June 2015 to do some *fun* math for an afternoon, I seized the opportunity immediately! However, it was slightly dismaying that mathematics was already being falsely partitioned into work vs. play. All mathematics—even the most rigorous proofs—is rooted in a narrative that involves endless play and joyful *struggle. In mathematics, this is not an oxymoron. It's a happy prerequisite.*

To walk into a grade 1 class was like starting teaching all over again. It was a completely different atmosphere—giggling students with attentive eyes and brimming smiles.

> After some nice introductions, I inserted a purposeful pause into my presentation, almost as though a magician was in the classroom. The test to see if my foray into number theory was going to pay hopeful dividends in terms of laughter and clapping came when I wrote the numbers 1, 3, 5, 7, and 9 on the board. I asked the class if anyone knew what kind of numbers these were. A few hands went up. One of the hands belonged

to my daughter, Raya. She had obviously forgotten that I told her that I would not be calling on her that afternoon. (I had told her in a positive way that she would know all the answers and that it would be nice to let other kids answer.)

I asked the girl sitting beside my daughter. Without breaking her smile—which was made cuter by some missing teeth—she uttered, "Odd." I smiled back and, with the enthusiasm of an animated clown, said, "That is correct!" She squeezed her hands in delight. This was a far cry from my high school classes . . .

Magic. In its most romanticized definition, it is where the doorways of mathematics are. These doors are literally found in the bright and colorful hallways of elementary school. Doors that lead into class-rooms that can quite easily accommodate the following sums:

$$1 + 3 = 4$$
$$1 + 3 + 5 = 9$$
$$1 + 3 + 5 + 7 = 16$$
$$1 + 3 + 5 + 7 + 9 = 25$$

The purposeful expulsion of our even numbers from our standard counting list to 10 leaves us with results that would *not* be recognizable to most young children. This is a good thing. Yes. *Good*.

Magic works because of the element of surprise. In mathematics, magic works *if* the surprising results are simple, triggering our intrinsic love for patterns. The numbers 4, 9, 16, and 25 (and so on . . .) are square numbers (2×2, 3×3, etc.). What we forget here is that they are literally square numbers! So . . . working backward, could those odd numbers be somehow building this square? Yes.

After the little girl labeled the numbers "odd," I then made a sheepish face and asked if anyone *knew* anything about the numbers 4, 9, and 16. A combination of silence and head shaking occurred, but the eyes remained glued to me—as though I was about to reveal the secret of a great magic trick! I could not have planned this any better. I sat down at the front table that was arranged for my presentation. Some of the kids sitting down at the front were curious as to what I was reaching for behind the desk.

I pulled out only one cube and put it on the table. I said, "One." I reached back and pulled out three cubes that were built to form a tiny letter *L*. I said, "Three." There was a tiny gasp from somewhere in the back. I reached back and pulled out the rest of these odd *L*'s. The class went nuts. Houdini was in the house. Sorry, *math* was in the house.

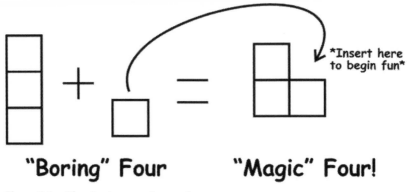

Figure 2.1.   Simple play equals surprise.

Doing the same activity, unfortunately, could elicit a similar response from high school students, as many will have never seen the physical construction of an odd number as the 12th letter of the alphabet. But, it is when you merge the simple but elegant mathematics with the laughing wonderment of a child that the authentic and lasting paths of learning get formed.

I picked up the one cube and fitted it snugly into the three. It not only gave the required answer of four that was on the board, but it made a *square*. I took this square and affixed it to the "waiting" five. This also made a square!

The classroom was going bonkers.

Adding consecutive odd numbers gives you square numbers. I did not have to ask the class if this was "neat." The grins resulting from tapping into the boundless joy of children were evident. What was even neater was that they had just witnessed the *physical construction* of a relationship that *if* revealed in high school, comes packaged in necessary abstraction/formulation.

$$1 + 3 + 5 + \underline{\hspace{1em}} + (2n - 1) = n^2$$

This is just the opening act. The main attraction of basic number theory, however, also harvests the numbers 1 to 10 with the accompanying plus signs. In fact, it is just the consecutive addition of those numbers. The italicization of the word *just* would be more than appropriate here, but in all honesty, would still not underscore how remarkably revealing mathematical simplicity can be.

FIFTY-FIVE

Fifty-five. What comes to mind right away? Maybe the speed limit that was imposed on US highways in the 1970s? (By the way, the late Texas mathematician Robert Moore had a mathematical proof that the safest speed to travel at was one that was about 10 percent over the speed limit.) Maybe it's the now-fabled retirement age? But, strictly in terms of playing with numbers, 55 conjures up perhaps an inert square from our times tables: $11 \times 5 = 55$.

Unfortunately, *playing* with numbers is something that rarely happens in schools. Remember, in the army they say you are treated like a number. That cold and hostile definition is a by-product of how numbers are presented in schools—dry and serviceable. Fifty-five also is one of the classic Fibonacci numbers, in which following numbers in the sequence are found by adding the previous two (2, 3, 5, 8, 13, 21, 34, 55 . . .).

Fifty-five has a historic simplicity that is connected a little more deeply to the first numbers we see and are physically intimate with. Fifty-five is the sum of the numbers from 1 to 10. And, it has a nice connection to 11×5.

1	2	3	4	5
10	9	8	7	6

A nice little wrapping/pairing activity gives us five sets of elevens. Numbers in elementary school should be approached with the ethos that is central to the cognitive and social development of children: simple play.

To top it off, in almost a literal sense, 55 looks like a number you might see at the grocery store. Really? Well, maybe a grocery store in the movies where they stack soup cans in a pyramidal fashion, only to have them be knocked down by the clumsy protagonist. Fifty-five is one of our triangular numbers for the simple reason that it can form a triangle!

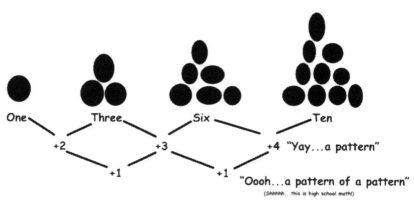

Figure 2.2.   The mathematics of handshaking.

So my opening act had gone extremely well. I knew now that the main attraction was going to be a huge hit. I asked the sitting kids to stand up and spread out. Without too much prompting, they were ready for something. In an inquisitive voice (as if I wouldn't even know the answer), I asked, "How many handshakes would there be if everyone shook hands with everyone once?" Without tempering the question with any caution of organization, I just let the class walk around and shake hands, while I counted in chaos and "put on" panic—obviously missing many handshakes.

The kids had a great time and they were amused by my antics. I then said, "Do you think there is any way to find out about how many handshakes happened?" Some said it was "impossible to count" or "it's too confusing!"

I then asked two kids to come forward. Shake hands. *One.* I then asked another kid to join them. We made sure everyone *met* each other through the physical and social gesture of shaking hands. *Three.* I then asked another kid to join them. Shake hands. "Make sure all four of you shook hands with one another," I said with a goofy sternness. *Six.*

CAN I SHAKE YOUR HAND?

Play is fun, but it also takes time. Sure, you can list the triangle numbers on the board with accompanying pictures of stacked marbles or soup cans, but nothing beats the personal discovery of patterns from excited students! A mathematician is simply, as I stated before, a pattern searcher. When kids go on field trips to something like a bakery, the learning and fun is enhanced when they are creating their own cake. In mathematics, that cake is just examining numbers in real-life situations *and* not-so-real-life situations.

A critical step—or a wall—that children need to see is that every level of thinking might have a barrier, or at least a fatiguing way of trying to calculate something. They will only want to explore something else if what they are using has difficulties that they personally see and experience.

At this point, I drew four dots and connected all of them with lines to "prove" the answer in a static, visual way. One kid then yelled out, "I know . . . let's draw 18 dots!" So, I draw 18 dots on the board forming a circle and start drawing lines. The faces are glued to this laborious activity for some odd reason. Then another kid said, "How long is this going to take?"

Bingo!

I said, "Way too long!"

There is a sense of satisfaction from the cheeky student to negate my demonstration. I politely ignored his commentary and drew five dots and connected them all with straight lines. The aesthetic of an inscribed star inside of a pentagon yields 10. I then wrote the distillate of all our hard work on the board.

1   3   6   10

Math needs to be messy, noisy, and confusing. It needs to be like the crazy kitchen in a restaurant where dishes are prepared—with trial and error, mistakes, challenges, and, hopefully, lots of fun. The nice plated meal that comes to your table is just the final part of the journey of this dish. The kitchen of mathematics is exploring and experimenting with numbers. To deny children this is to deny children mathematics. They need to learn how to *cook*; not just be *served*. How many handshakes will there be if there are 11 people in a room? Just follow the pattern of triangle numbers . . . 55!

Next time you are at a wedding or a large function, ask someone you are standing beside, "How many handshakes will there be for everyone to introduce themselves to all the people in the room?" If they haven't walked away from you after that math question, they might follow up with one of their own: "I don't know. *Do you?*" At this point, you would simply smile and say, "A big %$# triangle number!" And—for effect—you'd walk away.

While it is nice to find such rich deposits of math gold in these simple examples of number exploration, it's doubtful you're convinced that all of mathematics is that simple! While yes, you would probably have to go get a degree in mathematics just *to understand* the questions posed in the famous Millennial problems—a cool one million dollars for cracking these mathematical nuts—most everything that you experienced in school was darn simple.

And, no, we're not going to go through every topic to prove that probably unbelievable statement, but we will focus on a topic that is the scourge of almost every one of us. It's where we might have unofficially "checked out" around the middle grades. Ladies and gentlemen, I present to you again . . . fractions! Not only fractions, but the perhaps grim memory of *dividing* fractions! If this book can convince you that this topic was eye-openly clear, then there is enough traction to believe that simplicity reigns over mathematics. For your entertainment, look at this:

$$4\frac{1}{2} \div 1\frac{2}{3}$$

(Side note: Why did we ever have to do these questions in the first place? When will we ever come across the need to share four and a half pies with two kids—one missing a third of their body?)

Anyways, let's carry on.

All of us learned how to do these questions in our early teens. Do you remember what was involved in the end? *Flip it and multiply.* But, before we get to the mathematical sorcery that punctuates division of fractions, there was an initial step of turning these *mixed* fractions into *improper* fractions. Oh boy. The chapter on *Laughter* is not until later, but the first step in getting this question correct is to do something that is "improper." Okay. Multiplying the denominator by the whole number in front and adding the numerator will give you this:

$$\frac{9}{2} \div \frac{5}{3}$$

At this point, the context and relevance of the initial question is receding away from all of us. And of course, it didn't help matters that the next step—cloaked in mystery—was a gimmicky, procedural one. *Flip the last fraction and then multiply.* Voila! You get your answer. Can't you just hear a teacher saying, "Now here, you try the next 29 questions on your own!" (Cue *Charlie Brown* groan).

$$\frac{9}{2} \times \frac{3}{5} = \frac{27}{10} = 2\frac{7}{10}$$

The best part is that while we eventually got the hang of the mechanics, nobody in the class had the foggiest idea *what* was going on or *why*! If you got the correct answer, it was immaterial as to what else was going on around division of fractions. In the entire history of education, three kids probably put their hand up and asked, "Why do you flip and multiply?"

Subconsciously all of us were thinking *I don't need to understand math; I just need to follow these rules.* Yes. Rules and procedures of Byzantine nature would be the staples all of us would dine on to survive our remaining years of mathematics. Alas, no plates were returned to the kitchen.

It didn't have to be that way. Mathematics is simple. Humans complicated it for reasons that are still unclear. Let's get back to the division problem. Think of each stick in figure 2.3 as always being equal to one. So how many sticks are below? Four and a half, right? Now hold on to something! How many individual squares are there? If you count all of them, you should get . . . 27!

What about in figure 2.4? One and two-thirds would be the answer with 10 total squares.

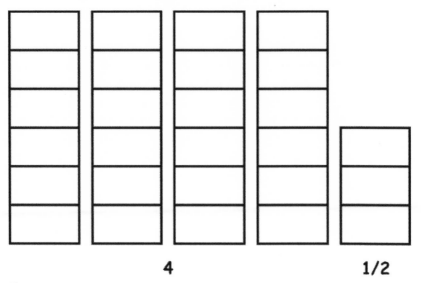

4   **1/2**

Figure 2.3.

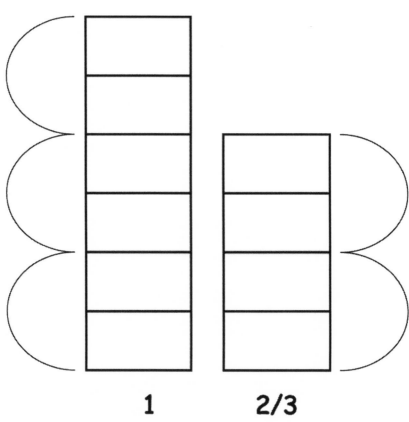

1   **2/3**

Figure 2.4.

What about the numbers 27 and 10? Were they not the numbers in our answer? Hang on, though. How did those numbers magically appear? Before we get to that, let's answer our question by looking at division in a way that might be new to you (a way you might understand!). Division can perhaps be looked at as *subtraction in disguise*. Yes. And, we have almost removed the mask—27 and 10. If you have $27 dollars in your bank account, *how many times* can you withdraw $10? You can only withdraw it twice, with a third attempt leaving you short. So, in the end, you can pull $10 out two times and you have seven dollars left, while you were trying to take out 10—2!

Wasn't that revelatory!? But, can you figure out where our needed numbers of 27 and 10 came from? Why did we make each stick with six blocks? You got it? Six is the common denominator for 2 and 3. Remember how we were told repeatedly that you can only add or subtract fractions if you have a common denominator? There you go! The mystery of fraction division solved. Well, yes and no. There is far more to discuss to examine what's going on here, but for the purposes of this book, we can stop right here.

It only gets better. You should have never have needed a calculator to do trigonometry and you could have learned the essential parts of calculus in grade 9. This is not a bluff! However, you would have needed practice examining simplicity in elementary and middle school. This involves lots of questioning—and time. Without a surplus of both crucial variables, the kitchen of mathematics becomes part of a fast-food emporium with poorly digestible items with tons of preservatives. Mathematics needs a *Slow Food Movement*!

In my entire 20-year career, never did I feel happier as a math teacher as I did in June 2015 when I realized the gateway for children to appreciate and love mathematics was the same one that had been around for thousands of years—the timeless beauty of numbers and their patterns. Their simple patterns. Simplicity is the underlying truth of all mathematics.

With patience, guidance, and yearning, it can always be revealed. We will explore many other imaginative areas of math, but it is crucial that we trust simplicity now. When we simplify our lives, and declutter all the things that are insignificant and meaningless, we become happier. We hear the sound of morning birds. We ponder over a still lake at dusk. We listen to the crackle of a dwindling campfire. These are all universal things that make us smile. Mathematics can only have that capacity if it is reduced to *its* chirps, ripples, and flames.

The magnificent world of mathematics was made for you. None of this magnificence would mean anything if it could not be seen by all of us. If it wasn't simple, it would not have brought so much happiness into my life. (I often remind myself to just "Keep it simple, Sunil!") And, if a small smirk escapes out of even the biggest skeptic, then maybe, just maybe, some of our simple pleasures in life might include math.

Q.E.D.[1]

Courage

> The enchanting charms of this sublime science reveal only to those
> who have the courage to go deeply into it.
>
> —Carl Friedrich Gauss

Proof. It's the bedrock of mathematics, but it requires a tenacity—and
yes, guts—to sometimes enter the darkest maze of this subject. Ironically though, since a sizeable portion of the population would shrink
away from the strange symbols and the exhausting rigor, the ideas of
perplexity, argument, and resolution are what attracts millions of readers to one of the most popular genres of fiction—murder mysteries.

The best murder mystery novels combine high-stakes tension with
a firm belief from the reader that they have the detective smarts to
crack even the most densely crafted case. Whether they can solve the
mystery is not as important as to believing they can. But, the reader
will not be impressed if even the tiniest of details was left out or seems
inaccessible. The whole book will have felt like a betrayal as not all the
information was available to the reader: "How was I supposed to know
that the murderer intentionally wore a shoe size three times too big!?"

The airtight solution to murder mysteries should feel like realization,
not revelation. The best way to arrive at a solution that doesn't deprive
the reader of a deflated ending is to ensure that it is a function of simple
logic. The Detection Club, a 1930s group made up of prominent British mystery writers such as Agatha Christie and G. K. Chesterton, had
to abide by an oath that was written by one of its members, Dorothy
Sayers:

Do you promise that your detectives shall well and truly detect the crimes presented to them using those wits which it may please you to bestow upon them and not placing reliance on nor making use of Divine Revelation, Feminine Intuition, Mumbo Jumbo, Jiggery-Pokery, Coincidence, or Act of God?

A little more than a half century earlier, Lewis Carroll would write one of the most famous and endearing books of all time—*Alice in Wonderland*. It has been a popular best seller despite it being in the challenging genre of nonsense literature. On first inspection, the genre literally sounds like a loose hodgepodge of ideas, but nothing could be further from the truth.

In literary nonsense, certain formal elements of language and logic that facilitate meaning are balanced by elements that negate meaning. These formal elements include semantics, syntax, phonetics, context, representation, and formal diction. It's a weighty offering that is necessary to keep all the sometimes clashing elements of writing in logical balance. Many of the arguments that occur in *Alice in Wonderland* were all based on Lewis Carroll's appreciation *and* lack of appreciation of mathematics. But, Lewis Carroll was merely a pen name for the stodgy academic, Charles Dodgson.

Charles Dodgson was a published mathematician in the fields of algebra and geometry. He was a devout follower of all things Euclidean, and probably kept a copy of *Euclid's Elements* on his night table. So, when mathematics was undergoing its own "industrial revolution" involving imaginary numbers and geometry, which was anything but the holy testimonials found in the second most published book of all time, Dodgson was not impressed. His mathematical conservatism was volleyed all over the place, but *Alice in Wonderland* offered a permanent and wider home for his stinging satire on the *nonsense* that he believed was going on in mathematics.

While there has been ample research into the social and political allusions of *Alice in Wonderland*, in 1984 Helena Pycior linked the trial of the Knave of Hearts with a Victorian book on algebra. Melanie Bayley, of the University of Oxford in England, has taken the analysis a lot further. She has described her findings—well, since we are in a chapter devoted to proof, we should say "theory"—in a piece called

Alice's Adventures in Algebra Wonderland Solved, published in *New Scientist*, December 16, 2009.

The ideas of logic have been in one of the bestselling books of all time, *Alice in Wonderland*, and one of the best-selling genres of all time. Logic is not just sober food for thought. It is also intrinsically captivating. And, it is a necessary precursor for the mother lode of perfectionist thinking—proof!

POWERFUL PROOF IN MOVIES

So, what you probably want to shout at this point is, *"Prove it!"* Uttering these simple words can create a wide variety of responses and emotions. One the one hand, it obliges anyone instructed to do so to raise the bar as high as possible to prove . . . *it*! In the 1997 movie *Contact*, based on Carl Sagan's book of alien contact, a minister named Palmer Joss (Matthew McConaughey) responds to the interrogative demands from astronomer Ellie Arroway (Jodie Foster) about the fundamental need for proof of God's existence. In a subdued but confident voice, Palmer Joss catches Ellie off guard with a personal question about her father, who had passed away when she was 10.

> *Palmer Joss*: [Ellie challenges Palmer to prove the existence of God] Did you love your father?
>
> *Ellie Arroway*: What?
>
> *Palmer Joss*: Your dad. Did you love him?
>
> *Ellie Arroway*: Yes, very much.
>
> *Palmer Joss*: Prove it.

There is no verbal response. Only a brief but heavy pause from Ellie, and her facial expression hints at a reexamination of perhaps the thankfully human boundaries of proof.

Love is not quantifiable and falls outside of the auspice of irrefutable logic. The courtroom, on the other hand, does not. Through our own knowledge—aided by books, TV shows, and films—we know the courtroom is the most famous arena where proof is demanded at a high level. And, just to underscore this demand, the burden of proof lies on the shoulders of the prosecution. Even still, even after all the reasoning and evidence is provided, a theoretically unbiased jury must decide the verdict.

Proof might be born in sterile objectivity, but it must pass through the human propensity of subjective bias—despite all the instructions issued by the presiding judge on a case. The best defense and prosecuting lawyers can only hope, after delivering flawless testimony, that the jury adheres to the adage *without a shadow of a doubt*.

In *12 Angry Men*, Juror #7, played by Henry Fonda, exhaustingly defends this central idea to liberty and justice. His arguments are persuasive, but impartial. Unlike most of the other jurors, he does not allow any bias, emotion, or self-serving agenda to interfere with cobbling together of the facts. In the end, all the collective hostility and anger toward him is diffused by a lengthy—but necessary—argument of clear and indisputable facts.

It is no wonder that this film is viewed as one of the great cinematic achievements. The movie, like Juror #7's case for innocence of the accused, is impeccable. So much so, that so many of the great individual performances get dwarfed by the victory for unrelenting logic.

That is how powerful compelling and intelligent proof can be. We can zero in on the art of persuasion, relegating even the most emotional, human performances to the sidelines. Sharpness in argument, free of temperance from blind faith and desperate hope, to convince and illuminate the most skeptical mind is the beautiful potential of our cognitive powers. Whenever it appears—in life and fiction—we take notice and applaud.

Unfortunately, even the idiom, *without a shadow of a doubt*, cannot be quantified. For what if one could have a doubt even smaller than this figurative guideline? *Whisper*? *Blink*? Those words seem strangely lighthearted when possibly dealing with the life of another human being. Yet, "shadow" is no better. It just has the traction of having been around in our language regarding uncertainty since the 19th century. There is never an absolute guarantee that truth will be paid handsomely with the correct verdict. In the end, it comes down to something that is both a human blessing and curse—hope.

There is, however, a standard of proof that goes well beyond what a courtroom could ever hope for. It will always have a 1.000 batting average—and all home runs. We are talking about *mathematical* proof.

THE BURDEN OF PROOF

If one would like to believe that God is a mathematician, then proof is God's poetry. Q.E.D. is Latin for *quod erat demonstrandum*. It is found at the very end of many mathematical proofs and philosophical arguments. It signals in no uncertain terms that whatever was needed to be proven has been proven. Often found in many academic writings during the Renaissance era, the notation has always carried some intellectual swagger. Whether it is a mathematical proof or some form of airtight reasoning, Q.E.D. is still the checkmate of the clearest thinking—that you are correct, the game is over, and the prize of irrefutable argumentation belongs to you.

Proof is the lifeblood of mathematics. It is not only where the greatest math stories are found, it is where mathematics keeps getting reborn and reawakened to its own magnificence. Proof is mathematics' wormhole to its own future, as each new proof catapults math into new adventures and frontiers. While many proofs become incubation chambers for societal applications, it is not why they are sought or cherished. Each new revelation—which often has been marinating in the collective minds of mathematicians for many decades—is its own simple triumph of peeling one more onion layer off the mathematical mysteries of the universe.

The casual phrase "prove it" wields a much more powerful force in numbers. It's mythological and often unintentionally tangential to divine thinking. It is not sufficient to cite one million cases where your idea works. No. It must work in the infinite arena of every case. Bridging that daunting gap, however, is not for the weak, as failure is what will most often greet you—over, and over, and over again. The Juror #7s of the mathematical world are rightfully lauded as noble warriors. The greatest mathematicians were not necessarily separated by ability; they were separated by courage.

THE REASON POEMS

Mathematical thinking can sometimes be exhausting. Thinking in isolation without notoriety or success is a recipe for emotional collapse—for almost everyone. In the Boston Marathon, around the 20-mile mark, there is a rather short ascent of only 88 feet that occurs over just under half a mile. However, this is a point in the race where the glycogen storage in muscles is most likely depleted—or what runners like to refer to as hitting *the wall*. Heartbreak Hill, just outside of Boston College, has been historically named because of how many runners basically succumb to this challenging climb.

The world of proof—especially the famous solved and unsolved ones—is *all* Heartbreak Hill. That is why the great 20th-century mathematician Paul Erdos surmised whimsically that all the great proofs must be in a book contained by God. Erdos called this book simply *The Book*. During a lecture in 1985, Erdos said, "You don't have to believe in God, but you should believe in *The Book*."

Like with everything in life, not everything is good just because it exists. It should be susceptible to being critiqued for pleasing aesthetics, and eventually gain universal approval—or disapproval. As such, not all proofs are treated the same.

Most people have some vague memories of doing those horrendously uninspiring two-column proofs where one had to prove one triangle was the same as another triangle. If that was your introduction to proof, then you should not be blamed for losing your appetite for not only proofs, but for mathematics as well.

> Instead of a witty and enjoyable argument written by an actual human being, and conducted in one of the world's many languages, we get this sullen, soulless, and bureaucratic form-letter of a proof.
>
> —Paul Lockhart

Even for those of us who feel they are good at math, proofs often represented the nadir of mathematics. Triangles that nobody cares about. Notation and formalization that reeks of some pedantic precision. If you could bottle this scent, it would have been called *eau du unnecessary surgery*, smelling of sterilized operating rooms. These proofs have become the bane of some of the leading voices in math education. Leading the charge has been Paul Lockhart, author of the seminal book *A Mathematician's Lament: How School Cheats Us Out of Our Most Fascinating and Imaginative Art Form*. Every math teacher should read that book before they start teaching!

Mathematics is an art form. If this is the case, the lifeless proofs that Lockhart refers to are paint-by-number. The best proofs are elegant because of their balance of creative genius and economy. They don't get into tiring tautological statements and head-spinning circular reasoning. They are creative enterprises of contemplation. Flailing at anything and rummaging for everything. Mathematics is hardly a sterile product. It's more than a noun. It's that bloody verb we mentioned earlier. And proofs are mathematical poetry—despite our dry and confusing experiences.

Nobody should be allowed to leave mathematics without having moments of struggle and emptiness—which are to be strangely embraced and valued. Even some bruising of an unhealthy ego would be good for the mathematical soul. Avoid the shortcuts and sterile elevators. Stay on the twisted path. Rest. Scrape the mud off your boots. Carry on.

Without giving people the experience of being a mathematician, we end up giving them a poor facsimile of mathematics. Worse, a failure of intersecting math without a complete human experience will occur—again. Like a formidable boxer giving a challenging one-two punch, let us bring back Lockhart to finish his knockout combo:

> Mathematics is the art of explanation. If you deny students to engage in this opportunity—to pose their own problems, to make their own conjectures and discoveries, to be wrong, to be creatively frustrated, to have an inspiration, to cobble together their own explanations and proofs—you deny them mathematics itself.

By that yardstick, there's been a lot of denial going on. Where for art thou, meaningful proofs? But, before we enter the sacred domain of world-class proofs and their intrepid curators, it is important to rewind the clock back to when we began school. Then, like with many of the topics left until high school, is when we should have got our feet wet with logic, reasoning, and proof. No triangles or dispiriting jargon! Only simple examination of endearing stories.

LOGIC IN NURSERY RHYMES

Charlotte Cutajar is a leader in math education in Toronto. Many years ago, she did a beautiful presentation on "Proof." She accessed as the start of the journey of logic and argument—nursery rhymes! The following is a nursery rhyme that we know all too well and was included in Cutajar's hefty handout:

> Jack and Jill went up the hill to fetch a pail of water. Jack fell down and broke his crown, and Jill came tumbling after.

But, for Cutajar, even a simple childhood story can serve as bedrock for logic and reasoning. Below are a few statements. Which ones are true and which ones are false? Which ones are just unfounded assumptions?

- Jack and Jill were the only two people who went up the hill.
- All people who go up hills fall down.
- Jack and Jill took a pail with them.
- Jack fell first then Jill.
- There was water at the top of the hill.
- The water spilled because of their falling.
- Jack and Jill were twins.
- Jack was angry at Jill.
- Jack and Jill fell because they went up a hill.

Suddenly there is curiosity and interest in discussing the validity of each of these events. Having children trying to defend or deny each statement related to a familiar context is where the long road to rigorous proofs should begin. Starting in high school with the equality plight of triangles is like giving kale to teenagers as their first serving of vegetables ever and expecting them to exclaim with joy, like Rachel Ray, "yummers!" No, this is not going to happen. And before you think that nursery rhymes have limited value in harvesting skills for deductive and inductive reasoning, Cutajar challenges us to recount the story of Hansel and Gretel:

> Hansel and his sister, Gretel, were lost in the woods. They walked and walked, and finally saw a lovely house made of gingerbread. Not knowing the house belonged to the witch, they walked up to the house and knocked at the door. No one answered the door, and they went inside. Being very hungry, they looked for something to eat. They opened the over door to see if there was any food inside, whereupon the witch sneaked up behind them and shoved them both in the oven.

Again, which statements are true and which ones are false?

- They were looking for food when they opened the oven door.
- Maybe Hansel was older than Gretel.
- Maybe Gretel was older than Hansel.
- It is possible that Hansel was older than Gretel.
- It is possible that Gretel was older than Hansel.
- It is impossible that they were twins.
- The gingerbread house was tiny.
- The witch was wicked.
- The gingerbread house belonged to the witch.
- The gingerbread house was in the woods.
- Hansel and Gretel were children.

Notice how there is an increased level of ambiguity now. However, that does not change the ability to assign truth or falsehood or assumption to any of the preceding statements. That is how we fold in proof into our children. Let them reason with the familiar, so they can naturally weave in their own interest to the fabric of proof. Once this is established, careful guidance—*hold on to the ropes, kids*—into reasoning ideas about numbers can take place.

At some point, *all* kids should see and marvel at one of the cheekiest proofs ever—the proof that there are an infinite number of prime numbers. For one, kids would learn about the building blocks of numbers, prime numbers—numbers that can only be evenly divided by 1 or itself. Two, the concept of infinity, which is usually a tough beast to slay, will be shown to be brought down in a few clever stabs of logical thinking. And, of course, three, highlighting how the idea to prove it for the general case is the end game . . . always. Case by case is not only impossible, but as will be seen, can lead to false conclusions.

THE MAGIC SWORD OF PROOF

The delightful framing of this proof is that it is found in the book that has never gone out of print in over 2,000 years and is rightfully considered one of the most important books in the history of the world—*Euclid's Elements*. Before we get to this proof—which is seen by many mathematicians as one of the most elegant and beautiful proofs in the history of mathematics—let's just remember how fundamental prime numbers are to creating every other number. Here are all the prime numbers under 100:

2, 3, 5, 7, 11, 13, 17, 19, 23, 29, 31, 37, 41, 43, 47, 53, 59, 61, 67, 71, 73, 79, 83, 89, and 97

Numbers go on forever. Prime numbers do as well. But, as an aside and a tasty appetizer for chapter 4 "Infinity"—are there more numbers or prime numbers? Our gut should tell us that there must be more numbers than prime numbers. Unfortunately, even the strongest gut instincts, well meaning and all, are not good traveling companions in trying to navigate the tricky trespass of infinity. It turns out that the *cardinality*—the number of "things" in a "set of things" is identical. They both contain an infinite set of numbers. No more and no less.

What?

Don't pop that aspirin yet! (Save it for the next chapter . . .)

In the first 100 numbers, prime numbers appear in healthy amounts—even beside each other (twin primes like 17 and 19, 41 and 43, and 71 and 73). However, they get rarer and rarer as you count. You might be counting forever. Hate to break this to you—you are not counting to infinity as if it's some mythical destination. It's *not* a number. As we shall shortly see, it means something bigger than a "mortal" number.

In most two-digit numbers, they appear 25 times. In other words, 25 percent of our childhood counting goal is made up of prime numbers.

Taking a giant and perhaps incomprehensible leap into numbers that are upward of 1,000 digits long, only 0.0004 percent of these will be the "magical" prime numbers. The rest—99.9996 percent—of the numbers will not be prime; these are known as *composite numbers*, and they are built with prime numbers.

While it appears that finding prime numbers in the stratospheric range of large numbers are extremely rare, they will go on forever. If you think of prime numbers as a heartbeat, primes seem to be full of life early on. We can hear their pulse often enough. But, as we move steadily toward infinity, there is almost deathly silence. And, only in the rarest moments do we get reminded that primes never die—they just get fainter, fading endlessly into the oblivion that is the endless sea of numbers . . .

There is a sweet sadness to this that plays right to our hearts. Things can be almost gone, but ironically always still there. It's the magic and mayhem of mathematics. So, when the largest prime number ever was found in September 2015, there was a small celebration in the math community. It has over 17 million digits!

In 1999, a cash prize of $50,000 was given for finding the first million-digit prime number. In 2008, the cash prize was doubled to $100,000 when the 10-million-digit barrier was cracked. (Not sure if Chuck Yeager even got a bottle of champagne for breaking the sound barrier . . .)

In case you're wondering, here are the first and last digits of this behemoth prime:

581887266232246442175100212113232368636370852325421 5893257 817044 . . . (17,425,042 digits omitted) . . . 682249493774541094283332309520370564565872574614198807172 4285951

Larger cash prizes will be given for cracking larger milestones. So, if you are a teacher, and some student in your class asks the legendary question of mathematical infamy—*when are we going to use this?*— borrow some stacks of hundreds, write the first 100 prime numbers, and tell students that a cool million might be available if they find a prime with a billion digits. Clear your throat and say, "Any more questions on when you will use math?" If the timing works out, a triumphant "class dismissed" would be a nice dramatic finish.

LET'S GET TO WORK

Okay, that was a nice diversion, but what about Euclid's masterstroke of brilliance to tame the beastly concept of infinite primes—especially since they become ocean pearls in the never-ending . . . end?

Warning: Mathematics Notation Ahead:
Please Slow Down . . . and Enjoy!

Step 1: Let's assume there are a *finite* number of primes.
Step 2: Let's attempt to contradict this statement—a much admired method called *Proof by Contradiction*.
Step 3: Let's create our finite list of prime numbers in such a way:

$$\{p_1, p_2, p_3, \cdots p_n\}$$

This list could be as big as we want, but it will have a last and final entry called p_n!

Now recall how we build new numbers with primes by multiplying them. For example, $2 \times 5 = 10$, $2 \times 3 \times 7 = 42$, $5 \times 7 \times 19 \times 71 = 47{,}125$, and so on and so on . . .

So, let's multiply all the primes on our list!

$p_1 \times p_2 \times p_3 \times \ldots \times p_n$ and (*cue small drum roll*) add a simple *1*. Let's call this number Q. What is Q besides being quite large and unknown?

Well, it's a coin-flip (albeit skewed) between it being prime or not being prime. We only have two choices! Well, what if it's prime? Well . . . uh-oh . . . it's *not* on our list of finite primes. Go ahead and check. There is no Q in our set. You just see a whole bunch of *p*'s. That's a problem.

Remember, if we contradict our initial statement of finite primes, then there must be an infinite number of primes. But, wait, we also have the option of it *not* being prime.

If it's not prime, then it must be built by prime numbers on our list. Our number $p_1 \times p_2 \times p_3 \times \ldots \times p_n$ will go nice and evenly into Q *if*

Q was p_1 x p_2 x p_3 x . . . x p_n, but it's not! Q is p_1 x p_2 x p_3 x . . . x p_n + 1. That innocent inclusion of "+ 1" messed things up for having a finite list of prime numbers! There is no combination of primes that will build our Q—we will always have one left over. So, Q cannot be built with our finite list of prime numbers. Our list is wrong. Our list is infinite. Q.E.D.

Mathematicians trip over themselves over this proof of infinite primes for the reasons already mentioned—it is elegant and compact. While the actual proof might not be of interest to the public, Euclid's crafty strategy is to be marveled. The very best lawyers have reasoning and logic skills that are rooted in mathematical proofs. The lawyers that ramble on and convince with solely emotional pleas tend to have far less persuasive powers than the ones that have a Euclidean sharpness.

But, you don't have to be in the legal profession to appreciate the mental gymnastics of mathematical proofs. No. The attribute to be persuasive with detached logic is a universal tool. Whether you are going into formal mathematics, the legal profession, construction, or even child-rearing, being armed with clarity and focus in your subdued arguments will save you precious time. You will also get less stress and headaches from creating or succumbing to discussions and debates that are light on facts, but heavy on yelling. That said, as a parent of two young children, I've found that the logic of children is non-Euclidean— Lewis Carroll should have written a parenting book as a follow-up to *Alice in Wonderland.*

THE SOULS OF REASON

In the early part of the 20th century, Bertrand Russell and Alfred North Whitehead, leading mathematicians *and* social thinkers of their time, wrote a book called *Principia Mathematica*. Fun title, no? Inside this book was a 300-page proof that $1 + 1 = 2$. That's right. No typos here. *Three hundred pages*. Most of the accomplished mathematicians have probably commented with something like "that sounds excessive"— despite understanding that *1*, +, =, and *2* needed rigorous definitions.

Less friendly folks would have said that Russell and Whitehead were a few axioms short of a full set. The least friendly—non-math people—are provided with a lifetime supply of hateful ammo toward math. If they would even catch a glimpse of just one of the pages of hieroglyphics found in this dense proof, it would probably make their dental fillings hurt.

Well, first, Modern Library places it 23rd on its top 100 nonfiction books of the 20th century. This is a list that includes heavyweight authors like Winston Churchill, Virginia Woolf, Booker T. Washington, Truman Capote, and Martin Luther King. (That ranking is even more impressive since there are *probably* only 17 people in the world who ever read *Principia Mathematica*.)

Principia Mathematica is not the kind of book that is part of a book club that meets every Thursday over wine and cheese. "Tonight, we are going to talk about the equal sign and the impact that it is having on one plus one. Sally, I know you have finished the book, but please don't give away the ending . . ." We could have fun with this all day.

This seems like an easy target—a 300-page book on the "obvious." Surely some of the perceptions people have about mathematics and mathematicians would be cemented here. Dour-looking men with scholarly names and turn-of-the-century photos—who seemed to be stiff reminders of the Victorian Age—engaging in this self-indulgent gibberish. That's what it would seem like until you knew something critical and generally overlooked about people like Bertrand Russell and Alfred North Whitehead—they were, well . . . *human*. In fact, in a way, their book is the *antithesis* of the rigidity that defines this ground-breaking proof.

All you need to know about Whitehead, besides that he was a great philosopher and mathematician, is his views on education. In a nutshell, this is it: "knowledge does not keep any better than fish." In other words, bits of disconnected knowledge are meaningless; all knowledge must find some imaginative application to the students' own lives, or else it becomes so much useless trivia, and the students themselves become good at just aping procedures and not creating their own thinking identity.

Whitehead also had one of the most romantic ideas about the purpose of the universe. He believed that the teleology of the universe was for the *production of beauty*. This poetic lens that Whitehead had must have influenced one of his most influential books, *The Aims of Education*. In 1916, Whitehead addressed some mathematicians in England. Parts of his speech would form the foundation for his groundbreaking book. The essence of his speech—and the book for that matter—is contained in one simple, powerful quote:

> Inert education is only not beneficial; it is dangerous.

Does this sound like a person who was cold and hard, as his famous proof might imply? In fact, it only gives the proof more intrigue and context as to the depths of rigorous imagination that our minds can go to. *Our* minds, not just *their* minds. Every symbol and notation that was carefully written was not only done with mind-boggling focus, determination, and precision, but also with rarely mentioned happiness. Oh, just you wait; there is *proof* of that later in this book.

The universal accomplishments of Russell and Whitehead should be celebrated and lauded with the same degree as any scientific, athletic, or artistic achievement. The mental stamina and endurance required to create these poems of reason is something that we might not comprehend, but we must appreciate and value. But, the depth of their rigor was a mere manifestation of the depth of their humanity. Deep plunges into one area of knowledge usually creates submersion into many other areas. Just look at all the great mathematicians of the Renaissance. Many pulled down night shifts as brilliant philosophers.

A NOBEL PUNK

Anthony Bourdain wrote of multiple passions in his book, *Les Halles Cookbook*. While the book offers tips on how to make classic French cuisine, Bourdain also offers life advice on where the passion for food takes him to passion for art, travel, and music. Getting excited about the minutiae of making something like a demi-glace only makes you excited and fascinated about other associated passions in life, implores Bourdain. Bertrand Russell was the Anthony Bourdain of the intellectual world. And not just for the myriad of passions and creations explored, but also for being a maverick . . . and a *punk*.

In 2005, I had the life-changing opportunity to teach at the International School of Lausanne on lovely Lake Geneva in Switzerland. Toward the end of the year, the English department put out its annual literary magazine—a collection of poems, essays, and artwork. Almost all the contributions were from students. A few were from teachers. Only one submission came from someone with a non-art background. That was me. I submitted an essay titled"Being Punk: Pursuing a Moral and Intellectual Life."

In the essay, I referenced many of my personal heroes and inspirations. Among them was Bertrand Russell. The definition of the word punk that I provided came from Glen Friedman, one of the most incredible photographers of my generation. His idea of the core of what it means to be punk was this:

An intense obligation to the truth of your innermost feelings.

Extracting the key words: an obligation to the truth of you . . .

Bertrand Russell. He is deserving of his own sentence. His *Wikipedia* page describes him as such: *philosopher, logician, mathematician, historian, writer, social critic, and political activist.* His antiwar stance put him in prison during World War I. He was an outspoken critic of Hitler and Stalin. In his later years, he attacked the United States for its involvement in Vietnam. He won the Nobel Prize in Literature in 1950. In 1927, he and his wife, Edith—who herself championed the intellectual and sexual freedom of women—opened a progressive boarding school called Beacon Hill. Bertrand Russell died in 1970, two years shy of turning 100. He lived a full life . . . and then some.

That's just it. Mathematics is not hatched in a vacuum or a sterile laboratory by one-dimensional people. The astronauts of logic and numbers will explore even the most distant and smallest crevices of mathematics with unimaginable detail. They will not do it despite being human—they will do it for the reassuring reason that they are *human*. Russell and Whitehead might have gone to an extreme of mathematical diction in *Principa Mathematicia*, but as the Indian mystic Osho said, "Courage is a love affair of the unknown."

The mathematical guts to go places that provide only the faintest hopes of resolution requires more than love of the subject. The kind of courage that needs to be extracted to tackle the hardest proofs in mathematics is almost unrecognizable. Most acts of courage, whether in war or personal battles with illness, get fully recognized just for fighting. The battles need not be won, which sadly occurs less often in these situations.

There is no medal of valor in mathematics for just trying as hard as you might. Already a lonely endeavor, most sojourns into the darkness of the unknown end up without a resolution. A few flickers of light. A door that won't open. Hallways that lead nowhere. That's the metaphoric reward of those who attempt to tackle the most stubborn of proofs.

None was ever more stubborn than Fermat's Last Theorem. Simon Singh wrote a magnificent story of this historical dilemma in 1998's *Fermat's Enigma*. We are familiar with the Pythagorean Theorem ($a^2 + b^2 = c^2$) where c represents the hypotenuse of a right-angled triangle. Figure 3.1 ($3^2 + 4^2 = 5^2$) is a clean and visually appealing relationship that dates to about 500 BC. While Pythagoras has been officially credited with this relationship of sides and squares, there is evidence that the Babylonians, Chinese, and Indians were also aware of this relationship.

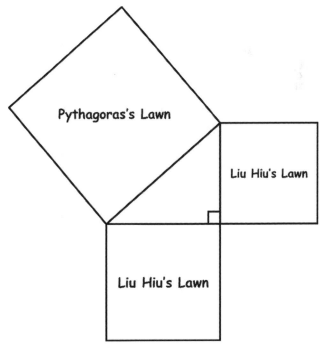

Figure 3.1.   Same amount of grass!

Of course, there are infinite solutions to the relationship, which are often referred to as Pythagorean Triples. Below are integer solutions to a, b, and c (c less than 100):

(3, 4, 5)	(5, 12, 13)	(8, 15, 17)	(7, 24, 25)
(20, 21, 29)	(12, 35, 37)	(9, 40, 41)	(28, 45, 53)
(11, 60, 61)	(16, 63, 65)	(33, 56, 65)	(48, 55, 73)
(13, 84, 85)	(36, 77, 85)	(39, 80, 89)	(65, 72, 97)

Go ahead—grab a calculator and check them. They all work. And, there are way more—an infinite set of them! But, Fermat had a curious revelation about this relationship. He wondered if there were any integer solutions to a, b, and c if the exponent was *bigger than* 2. What if the exponent was 3? 4? 17? 1,309? How bizarre to have king's ransom of solutions for the exponent being 2 and then to . . . not have any solutions for any exponent bigger than 2?

Fermat's gut said in the endless sea of possibilities of exponents there would never be a solution to $x^n + y^n = z^n$ for n greater than 2. He said he had a proof of this, but it was too large to fit in the margins of the pages of the book he was reading, *Arithmetica*, a heralded primer on number theory written by the Greek mathematician Diophantes around 250 AD.

Now Fermat was a clever chap, but many doubt he had the mathematical ingenuity to have proven this. The biggest reason for this doubt is that after he proposed the problem, a solution was not found for over 300 years. It's not that nobody cared. *Au contraire*! The proof became all consuming for generation after generation after generation of mathematicians.

With the passage of time, the impenetrability of this proof only hardened. And while the result of everyone who attempted to find a counter-example (i.e., an integer exponent bigger than 2 that happened to work) or a general proof *always ended in failure*, this did not discourage the brightest number theorists from making courageous attempts.

THE ANSWER MUST BE IN THE ATTEMPT

In 1995 Richard Linklater directed the movie *Before Sunrise*. In it, a young French woman named Céline (Julie Delpy) and an equally young American man named Jesse (Ethan Hawke) spend a whole day together, walking and talking through the streets of Vienna. In the wee hours of the morning, there is a scene in a deserted alleyway in which Celine is trying to make sense of the meaning of life in the subtlest of ways. She utters one of the most eloquent lines ever said regarding humans and communication:

> I believe if there's any kind of God it wouldn't be in any of us, not you or me but just this little space in between. If there's any kind of magic in this world it must be in the attempt of understanding someone sharing something. I know, it's almost impossible to succeed but who cares really? The answer must be in the attempt.

The answer must be in the attempt. In mathematics, not only does the answer lie here, but so does everything that it embodies. The solution, while crucial—especially for advancing mathematics (hence, society)—is merely the result of how and why we get there. Simply to try and exert effort for no other reason than to share in the communicative processes of being alive and curious—that is where we find math's magic.

And no other proof in history has carved out such lore as Fermat's Last Theorem. It became *The Amazing Race* for mathematics. Unfortunately, there would be no victors in the problem that only had its legendary stance heightened by stories of despair, intrigue, rivalry, cash awards, suicide, and death.

A heartwarming story that is emblematic of what the power of mathematics holds in terms of happiness is found in one of the thousands of people that went head to head with Fermat's Last Theorem. The story is richly told in Simon Singh's brilliant *Fermat's Enigma*. Sometime toward the end of the 1800s, Paul Wolfskehl, a German industrialist and amateur mathematician, was on the point of suicide. According to some historians, the spiraling depression was the result of either failing health through multiple sclerosis or a failing heart through a dying romance; others believe it was due to the onset of multiple sclerosis. He even set a date for his suicide and intended to shoot himself through the head at midnight.

Like some Hollywood twist of fate, Wolfskehl visited the library and began reading about the latest research on the Last Theorem, the time he'd set for his suicide only hours away. While reading the book, he suddenly believed he—like thousands before him—had inroads to the solution. He became completely entangled in his newfound belief. But, after a few hours of dabbling in his strategy, he came to the same place that far too many had come to before—a dead end.

There was, however, a silver lining that was beginning to unfold. Midnight had passed, the appointed time of the solution to his despair. It was in this emotional abyss that he was reminded of the timeless beauty of mathematics. His debilitating health and broken heart became no match for the joy that resurfaced at the most critical period of his life. He was happy again.

Impending death was not staved off by counseling from friends; it was staved off by an almost narcotic immersion into mathematics. Mathematics had renewed his desire for life. The interface between the gravest form of depression and personal salvation was not something visible and concrete. It was the chemical reactions happening in the brain. Neurotransmitters, endorphins, axons, and synapses. Everything working naturally and enthusiastically in ways that are both accountable and ineffable. *Life's splendor no longer had to wait for Wolfskehl.*

So grateful was Wolfskehl to the problem that saved and renewed his life that he offered a prize equivalent to $2 million in today's money to whomever could pull the sword out of this mathematical rock. He received over 600 responses. None of them were correct.

By the middle part of the 20th century, with Fermat's Last Theorem now past its 300th anniversary of irresolution, many believed that the planet would annihilate itself in nuclear Armageddon before a solution would ever be found. Computers began to confirm that Fermat was indeed correct as they started showing that even exponents that are 1,000 digits long will not provide a solution that satisfies the relationship to $x^n + y^n = z^n$.

However, as impressive as that might be, it does not constitute a proof, only a strong hunch . . . at best. By the early 1960s, a doorway would open up in the most unlikely places—elliptical curves. There is no need to detail this road other than that the most difficult problems in mathematics will eventually—often at the speed of erosion—lead to surprising connections with other branches of mathematics. In time, these branches fuse and give birth to new mathematics.

One of the most disheartening perceptions of mathematics is that it is "all discovered." Well, it would take about 80 books to cover all the mathematics that had been discovered up until the beginning of the 20th century. Now? It would take 100,000 books! A person who would add to this growing compendium of mathematical knowledge would be Andrew Wiles—the hero who would eventually stun the world in 1993 with a solution to Fermat's Last Theorem.

In 1963, Andrew Wiles borrowed a book from a local library in Cambridge, England. The book was called *The Last Problem* by Eric Temple Bell. As suggested in the title, the book was a 300-year look back at the most important unsolved problem in mathematics. Wiles's fascination with Fermat would only be amplified for the rest of his life, unwittingly, however, to the point of a nervous breakdown—the too-often punctuation mark of such intense devotion.

Seven years of isolation eventually led to a solution, which was announced to the world in the quietest of fashion on June 23, 1993. The silence lasted only minutes, as this stunning revelation was communicated throughout the world, eventually making headlines in the *New York Times* and *People* magazine.

Mathematical proof has incredibly high standards that are unsympathetic to time or brilliant hunches or to computers showing a billion cases where it works. Wiles's 150-page proof, a light read compared to Russell and Whitehead's *War and Peace* proof of $1 + 1 = 2$, met with standards that, as Erdos might have said, God's approval.

However, having mathematical chops—as great as they might be—will only give you a ticket to watch the marathon. But, if you choose to run, then you have already won. The restorative powers of mathematical thinking at the highest degree offers a cleanse that only those who have *attempted* to join the ongoing race in mathematics can describe.

All proofs are born out of crisis. That is the only reason to begin the long haul of justification. It's where our intuition and imagination are stymied, and everything starts to run counter to what we dearly believed. It is in this desperation that a deep sigh and a complete collection of our thoughts are required. Being "dead wrong" is the seed that all great mathematicians—and thinkers and innovators in general—must be blessed with early on to develop the stamina for proof.

Without such crisis, mathematical exploration would come to a halt. You see, sobering failure of initial instincts is the engine that drives the richest journeys in mathematics. And, like all good journeys, the story will be more than just the destination—which in math is often a very delayed flight with turbulence—but the hundreds of stops along the way, each a colorful component of the human experience.

Very few of us have the courage to take these failings of the heart, mind—and yes, soul—to the darkness that awaits. And yet, as history has proven, the finding of the elusive light—*if* it exists at all—is not what illuminates these rare individuals. No. It's merely the search.

It's perhaps even less than that. It's merely *the attempt*—a most humble option—as wistfully said by Julie Delpy's Céline in a movie about love.

Mathematics is also a love story. Its running time is a few thousand years—and counting. The answers have been dwarfed by questions. The resolutions have been eclipsed by failure—with failure now needing to be redefined as joyful struggle.

They say that the end justifies the means. For mathematics, the end—courageous devotion to the truth—*defines* the means. And that is enough light for all of us.

NOTE

1. Q.E.D. (sometimes written "QED") is an abbreviation for the Latin phrase "*quod erat demonstrandum*" ("that which was to be demonstrated"), a notation that is often placed at the end of a mathematical proof to indicate its completion. Eric W. Weisstein, "Q.E.D." Wolfram MathWorld. http://mathworld.wolfram.com/QED.html (accessed December 13, 2016).

CHAPTER 4

Infinity

Curiosity

> Look up at the stars and not down at your feet. Try to make sense
> of what you see, and wonder about what makes the universe exist.
> Be curious.

> —Stephen Hawking

Twinkle, twinkle, little star. How I wonder where you are. Such are the
timeless and recognizable words of the 200-year-old English lullaby.
However, while the poem has five stanzas, only the opening one is well
known. But, even in those short and simple words that speak with the
delight of a child, the essence of our finiteness and place in the universe
is magically captured.

On the clearest night, stars are always a stunning reminder of not
just our dizzying place in the cosmos, but of our shared picture of the
night sky with the millions of humans who have come before us. Jane
Taylor's poem "The Star" might have been written in the early 19th
century, but its intention for us to ponder on the faintest pulsations of
light that the universe has to offer has been around since the beginning
of time.

Current estimates put the total number of galaxies at 10 trillion. Using our own Milky Way galaxy as a guide, that would put the number
of estimated stars in the universe at around 100 *octillion!* That is a
number that contains 29 zeros. Big numbers exist because, while we
may be small, our minds are not.

Back to our clearest night—or darkest sky, free of urban light
pollution—for a moment. How many stars can you see with the

unaided eye on the most romantic night? The answer might surprise you. It is under 5,000. To be eerily precise, the number is 4,548. Dorrit Hoffliet of Yale University compiled this number a decade ago using the idea that the naked eye limit of seeing stars from Earth was a magnitude 6.5. With that reference, the total number of stars visible in the hemispheres of our planet is 9,096. Since we can only see one hemisphere at a time, that number must be halved.

There seems to be this contradictory feeling of smallness and largeness in all these facts. A beautiful night sky can shower us with a dazzling light show and inspire the most profound pieces of poetry and thought. And yet, in the grandest scheme of things, we witness light events of the universe that are only an octillionth of what goes on every day.

Every day for billions of years the universe has put on a show for pretty much nobody. There is a math equation called the Drake formula that calculates high estimates of intelligent life elsewhere. A slight pang of existential loneliness might be creeping in now. But don't despair! Mathematics can quantify our alienation from the universe to make us truly understand our smallness. The consolation is not in feeling small but, rather, in seeing things big!

BIGGER THAN GOOGOL

The world's largest number? What does that mean? Sure, numbers go on and on and on . . . but don't humans just stop labeling or describing them after a while? Googol is big. One hundred zeros. Not sure what the use of it could ever be, but it has traction in our pop culture now. Thanks to *Google*. This is not the only strange number Google tried to help popularize. In a mysterious, Yoda-like voice, proclaiming the existence of another one—we'll dive into Google's attempt at publicly paying dues to this magical number later in the book.

But, there are numbers bigger than Googol. Numbers so big that even the universe cannot contain them! However, let's pretend we are on a tour of a fictitious *Museum of Numbers*, so the really big one is at the end of the tour. The room we are currently in houses all those *illion* numbers—million, billion, trillion, etc. In a season 10 episode of *The*

Simpsons, Mr. Burns is in possession of a trillion-dollar bill—a bill that was produced by Harry S. Truman to help rebuild Europe following World War II. In a strange twist of rare life imitating art, Zimbabwe printed a trillion-dollar bill in 2009 due to hyperinflation. It was worth about 30 US dollars. "Don't go spending that all in one place" was not applicable here.

The largest of the *illions* is the number centillion with 303 zeroes. But, nobody uses any of these numbers—even a trillion is rarely used. That is because scientific notation—10 raised to whatever exponent your heart desires—is the adopted and generally well-understood convention for discussing large numbers (and small numbers for that matter).

It seems almost pointless to go beyond, as the discussion of every imaginative contemplation of largeness is less than a centillion. For example, a drop of water contains 6 sextillion atoms—a number that has 21 zeros. The total number of hydrogen atoms in our universe *only* contains about 81 zeros. The number closest to that in the *illion* family is the number vigintillion, with 63 zeros. Aren't we kind of done here, then? Counting hydrogen atoms in the universe just sounds like a great way to kill a Sunday afternoon!

On the popular YouTube channel VSauce—which now has three separate channels with a total of over 15 million subscribers—the Internet host of hosts, Michael Stevens, took a plunge into the mind-blowing scope of finite numbers in the episode "Will We Ever Run out of New Music?" VSauce videos are relatively short but high energy. They are the protein bars of information and contemplation. In this episode, the quasi-alarming question is disarmed by the sobering magnitude of how many different songs can be created.

A five-minute song involves storing information as bits—either as 1s or 0s. A song of this length as Michael proclaims—with a somewhat exhaustive tone—is on the order of 211 million bits. So, the total number of possibilities in a five-minute audiophile is:

$$2^{211\ 000\ 000}$$

This number is insanely large for a reason. It not only contains all the possible songs of this length that could ever be made, it contains—as the animated host of VSauce tells us—every five-minute conversation in the history of the world! And, if that doesn't implode your brain like the demolition of a cheap Vegas hotel, then this additional fact might: also contained is every conversation that *never* happened.

The number of hydrogen atoms in the universe might seem like the limit of finite madness, but this number, when unpacked from its scientific notation form, is a number that is 63 million digits long. As we are going to see, even the universe is too small to discuss some finite numbers. Much too small . . .

On page 147 of the 1977 *Guinness Book of World Records*, there is a piece of print—the size of a fortune inside one of those delectable Pac-Man-shaped cookies—that states the record of records. For a wide-eyed 13-year-old, it might as well have been poster sized. Here was the record of the largest number ever used in a mathematical proof—Graham's Number. It had an explanation/notation with upward pointing arrows and seemingly narcissistic Gs. I didn't understand it then and I barely understand it now. My love for math was born in chaos not clarity.

GRAHAM'S NUMBER

Graham's Number has several videos on Numberphile—the social media darling of all things hot'n heavy in number theory. One of the videos is Ron Graham himself trying his best to explain his *own* number—which is some hellish iteration of exponentiation. For example, 5×10 versus 5^{10} creates quite a gulf when comparing multiplication with exponentiation. Similarly, exponentiation and the *exponentiation* of exponentiation results in an accelerated gap between these two numerical results.

Graham's Number, which is the result of an innocent-looking question involving connecting dots in a square with two different colors, rapidly descends into such madness that the hosts of Numberphile made a video just reacting to its monstrous size. One of the reasons for this is the warp speed at which this number travels. How does a square *turn into* a cube? Quite simple, really. You just move it through space and then connect the dots. A square with four dots and six possible lines now is a cube with eight dots and 28 possible lines.

Can you move a cube through space? Sure can! And after you do, connect those dots—quite a few now—and you will have created the magnificent hypercube, the *tesseract*. If you Google this object, you will see that it has many nested cubes, in much the same way a cube has its recognizable squares (the faces). But, the image you will be staring at will only have one color in all its lines/struts. Furthermore, if you connect all the possible vertices of the tesseract with lines, you would have a total of 120 of them—each of the dots connected to every other dot.

But, what if you could choose between two colors? How many *different looking* tesseracts could you make? Would you believe an astronomical 2^{120}! Quick, go to the cupboard and grab your ibuprofen—you are going to need it. The whole notion of this *thing*—remember there was a classic horror movie called *The Thing*—involves two colors, avoiding a certain color combination, and traveling into the 13th dimension.

The cheeky folks at Numberphile even have a video in which they semi-jokingly think that contemplating the size of Graham's Number could turn your head into a black hole. Nobody knows how many digits are in this number, and the only thing that even Ron Graham knows about his numerical Frankenstein is that it . . . ends in a seven. If each digit of Graham's Number was written the size of a hydrogen atom and you had a piece of paper the size of the observable universe, guess what? You still would not have enough room to write this number.

So, in the spirit of nobody's brain reaching a density of a cosmological event, let's move on. Let's boldly go where so many have gone—that final frontier of numbers: infinity.

THE PROBLEM WITH INFINITY

To truly appreciate the numerical and almost psychological impact of infinity, it was crucial that you be presented with the headache of the largeness of some of the ways to count things—hydrogen atoms in the universe, number of different conversations in the time it takes to boil an egg, and some vaguely explained coloring activity involving a journey through multiple dimensions and possible brain explosion/implosion.

What doesn't kill you makes you stronger. Isn't that what they say? Well, congratulations, you're on your way to being the Marvel character of your choice. *Mr. Fantastic*, holder of five doctorate degrees (including math) would be a solid choice!

In all seriousness, infinity—when you stop and think about it—shouldn't be something that humans are capable of assimilating into their lives. For most of us, the goal line of thinking in big numbers invariably involves wealth and money. A million dollars has a universally recognized equivalence of freedom and luxury. Billions and trillions has comprehension as well in terms of hyper-wealthy or country debts and deficits. All the numbers mentioned so far, that rip by these pedestrian offerings like a Porsche 944 on the Autobahn, don't have an intrinsic intersection in our lives.

It's not that the numbers are too big; it's maybe that our lives are too small—that sometimes staring into the abyss of mathematics can yield butterflies and goose bumps. You know, those moments that yield those figurative gasps for air. That's mathematics at its most mind-boggling best. Yet again, let's look to the words of (Sir) Paul Lockhart for clarity:

> Mathematics is the music of reason. To do mathematics is to engage in an act of discovery and conjecture, intuition and inspiration; to be in a state of confusion—not because it makes no sense to you, but because you gave it sense and you still don't understand what your creation is up to; to have a break-through idea; to be frustrated as an artist; to be awed and overwhelmed by an almost painful beauty; to be alive, damn it.

The most important word in that quote is "alive." This is what mathematics is—a living and glowing creation in our universe *because* of our universe. The practicality of mathematics is that it beautifies our vista far more than making our daily tasks easier or understandable. Mathematics should leave you with blissful stains in your life.

Don't misunderstand—when mathematics wants to be a Clydesdale workhorse, it can deliver the goods, making so many functioning ideas of society easier to comprehend. But, hopefully, life is beyond the practical borders of duty, chores, work, and obligation. Well beyond. It is there you will find mathematics. And, in the outer limits, in the Twilight Zone—*literally*—you will come across infinity.

INFINITY AND POP CULTURE

The Twilight Zone had many of its story lines involving some freakish malleability of time. Sometimes it stopped. Sometimes it went backward. Sometimes it got caught in a loop. Twice it went on forever—speaking loosely, infinity. Rod Serling must have had some knowledge of the tormenting power of infinity as the two characters that were ostensibly gifted eternal life—the closest human application of infinity—are fatigued by their immortality. In the season 1 episode titled "Long Live Walter Jameson," the title character is a history teacher who is lauded by his students for his almost uncanny detailing of historical events. That is because he is several thousand years old and cannot die.

Eternity is not a peaceful adventure, and living for a couple millennia had ironically become a prison for Serling's character. Several years later, one of the most popular science fiction series of all time, *Riverworld*, would have a deep philosophical discussion among some of its central characters on such longevity toward the end of its last book. Since the premise of *Riverworld* is about everyone who has ever lived being resurrected on this mysterious planet, it is only fitting that the final conversations revolved around everlasting life. However, in the book, the wise Sufi character Nur believes that humans are not ready for eternal life—that their brains have not developed to handle the enormity of living forever.

Art has told us that infinity is something not to be entertained lightly. When it comes to wishing for the mythical fountain of youth, we should be careful. And yet, some of the best insights on infinity have come from authors who paint a lighthearted door for understanding this concept.

In Brian Clegg's marvelous book, *Infinity: The Quest to Think the Unthinkable*, the kindergarten number rhyme of *one two, buckle my shoe* graces the pages very early on. Sure, the book eventually folds in mathematical nomenclature to properly detail what infinity is, but Clegg and companies like Pixar are smart enough to understand that infinity starts with childhood marvel and delight:

> To infinity and beyond!
>
> —Buzz Lightyear

The night sky. Twinkling stars. Eternal life. Childhood wonder. That is ample evidence that infinity exists for us to ponder and wonder—to have the warmest and most natural installation of curiosity in our lives. While one of the most challenging ideas in all of mathematics to comprehend, early adventures with infinity are accessible to all of us.

Curiosity is far more than just a universal trait for probing—mischievous or otherwise—it is a primal activity that needs to be exercised with the same attention and routine as our physical maintenance. In Ian Leslie's book, *Curious*, the lengthy subtitle hints at such importance: *Curious: The Desire to Know and Why Your Future Depends on It.* Curiosity is not a gift for the cognitive elite, it is something to be cultivated daily into everyone's lives.

Infinity and its contemplation is the oldest ritual for nurturing curiosity that humans know. Aside from some mental anguish, it is also much safer than eating bugs, playing with matches, and venturing into dark caves—all activities initiated by childhood curiosity. Unfortunately, 19th-century mathematician Georg Cantor—the inventor of set theory—would be tormented and ridiculed for his illuminations of infinity.

Almost playing out like some dark tale of isolation and madness, one of Cantor's historic finds in his descent into uncharted mathematical territory would be his . . . *monsters*. There was no exaggeration here. These numbers literally broke the mathematical plane with their ambiguous nature and bizarre behavior. One of the first monsters was created from a tactical and repetitive removal of one-third of a line. He repeated this process for an infinite amount of times. The first few lines of this recursive process look like this (figure 4.1):

Figure 4.1. Cantor's first monster.

What Cantor created here was an infinite number of lines with an infinite set of points—something bigger than infinity. His mind—as teenagers might say—was *blown*. This monstrous creation led Cantor, unfortunately, to a sanatorium. As we will see in the next chapter, these monsters would alter the landscape of mathematics in the 20th century . . .

WHAT REALLY IS INFINITY?

Curiosity is a natural and primal enhancement of our mental lives. Simple translation: It is a vessel for happiness. Numbers can exhaust us. Heck, they can even frighten us. But, that is all okay. To be overwhelmed is to inhale and exhale with the exhilaration that Lockhart sees as paramount to being emphatically alive—with mathematics.

Google the word *infinity*. Sure enough, you will get many images of that iconic sideways eight symbol. Interspersed with these images will be the odd piece of jewelry that has the word "love" fashioned into this *lemniscate*—the algebraic name for this beautiful curve.

Many would argue the strongest love that can possibly exist is that between a parent and their child. Ask a mother or father to try and quantify this love to their child and it usually *starts* in the passage from the book *Guess How Much I Love You.*

As mentioned in the previous chapter, love is thankfully not quantifiable. It then makes perfect sense for it to be linked to infinity. People might have an initial aversion to the mathematical probing of infinity, but most of them are quite familiar with the boundless nature of the most treasured human expressions: love and curiosity.

One of the most common misconceptions is that infinity is a number, found way, way, way out there at the end of a number line. It's not. That is why, technically speaking, it's not often used in its correct context. As mentioned in the last chapter, infinity is a measure of how many numbers there are. It describes a set of things. The difference might appear subtle, but it's not. Thinking that infinity somehow behaves just like large numbers—centillion, googol, googolplex, and Graham's Number—is what gets us into trouble.

Imagine, if you will, that you have a barrel. And you are on the clock. Specifically, 60 seconds. In the first 30 seconds, your task is to dump ping-pong balls numbered 1 to 10 into this barrel, and before that allotted time is up, retrieve ball number 1. Chopping your time in half, you now have 15 seconds to dump balls 11 to 20 and retrieve ball number 2. Continuing with this kind of game show challenge, you are now down to 7.5 seconds to dump balls 21 to 30 and, yes, retrieve ball number 3. Let's assume you have the superhero powers of the Flash and are not constrained by the continuing halving of time. At the end of 60 seconds, how many balls are in the barrel?

Before you answer, you should know that this is a collision of three different sets of infinity—the balls going in, the balls coming out, and the time intervals. This bouillabaisse of infinity conundrum is a tasty soup of utter confusion! Confusion, as has been alluded to directly and indirectly, is a wonderful thing in mathematics. It is a natural state of mathematical thinking and has been responsible for giving color and texture to the historical development of mathematics.

Confusion needs to have a desk in all the math classrooms. It needs to be an animated student that motivates the classroom to value mistakes, errors in thinking, and wrong turns. How does it go again? *To err is human, to forgive divine.* How about to err is human, to do math divine. Confusion is the trail of bread crumbs in truly appreciating infinity. Without experiencing the frustration of the rough terrain of this mental hike, infinity would be such a limp excursion.

The clash of the infinities in the ping-pong ball dilemma above usually results in answers with complete lack of confidence—total confusion. Infinity's temperament is precisely to create chaos and conflict. Comfort and clarity? *Pffft!* That's for numbers—finite and mortal. Immortality doesn't come cheaply in math. Ante up some native curiosity, patience, and a necessary anguish, and *one* of the holy grails in math is yours for the taking.

> I would rather have questions that cannot be answered than answers that cannot be questioned.
>
> —Richard Feynman

THE PING-PONG BALL DILEMMA

We are often poked and prodded to leave our comfort zones in life. Try something new. Travel to new destinations. Pick up a new hobby. Make that jump to a new job, new experiences . . . new life. For some, the jump is easier. For others, it's a struggle. Both are almost irrelevant. The purpose is not for a soft or hard landing; the purpose is to jump.

Remember? It's all about the *attempt*. It is where the nectar of life is. It's never really been about the answers. It's been about the questions. Desiring contemplation is all that matters. Whether that leads to being confused or comforted is almost immaterial. Answers can only exist if questions are posed. Questions can only be posed if we are curious.

And historically, nothing has been more inviting than infinity. The ping-pong ball problem has been circulating the Internet for a while now, with some of the biggest names in mathematics taking whimsical stabs at trying to untangle infinity for all of us. *Plus Magazine*, one of the oldest and most colorful websites in expounding all that is math, framed the problem with a lighthearted story line of Batman and Superman, cleverly seeing that superpowers are needed to withdraw balls in intervals of time that will become *illionths* of seconds shortly.

So, how many balls are left in the barrel in the end? Zero. A result that is counterintuitive and confusing, and yet, more fun than a barrel of monkeys! How can there possibly be an empty barrel? Weren't we putting more balls in the barrel than taking out? Yes, but pick any ball. Ball 17, 528, 29,781,015 . . . Graham's Number—they all will have been pulled out at some point before the 60 seconds is up.

The key to reconciling this mathematical weirdness is to remind ourselves that infinity refers to the number of things in a set of things and the correspondence of these sets with each other.

Set A: The infinite sequence of time intervals (½, ¼, ⅛, . . .). Each dumping of balls results in the remaining time to be halved, and then halved again. And so on. The key thing is that there is an upper bound of 60 seconds. The experiment will be finished after one minute.

Set B: The infinite number of balls removed (1, 2, 3, . . .). What is critical about this set is that it shares an important one-to-one correspondence. Every interval of time, which we have an infinite amount of, matches up perfectly with every ball removed. If the number of time intervals is the same as the number of balls removed—infinite—then when this chaotic minute is over, there will be exactly zero balls left in the barrel.

While this should offer some insight into how infinity behaves, it's not even the beginning of where it goes. Buzz Lightyear's line in the first *Toy Story* ("to infinity and beyond!") was not only catchy, it was mathematically correct—he just didn't describe how "beyond" should be properly denoted. For what he really was saying was "infinity plus aleph-naught." Even more interesting, what Buzz was obliviously saying to millions of kids watching is that yes, yes you can count *past* infinity!

So, in the spirit of this chapter—to stoke the fire of curiosity through the door of infinity—this is where it ends *and begins* for you. How does one leapfrog over infinity? What more mathematical juggling, gymnastics, and magic tricks are going to be seen now? Your journey might lead you to people like Zeno and Cantor but, more than likely, land at the golden temple of curiosity—the very hot and spicy VSauce. Gaining heavy traction in classrooms with students and teachers due to the engaging freneticism of host Michael Stevens, VSauce now inspires millions to fall down rabbit holes and chase down questions like "What is the speed of *dark*?"

There has never been a more fertile period to unravel the greatest mysteries in our universe. Infinity might be on edge as a mathematical construct, but as an idea for nurturing curiosity and having mathematics become inclusive in our daily discussions, infinity is the epicenter. We've explored infinity in this chapter. Now the onus is on you to heed the call of Buzz Lightyear—and go beyond!

CHAPTER 5

Negative Square Root

Gratitude

> The moment one gives close attention to anything, even a blade of
> grass it becomes a mysterious, awesome, indescribably magnifi-
> cent world in itself.
>
> —Henry Miller

Do you remember your first calculator? Regardless of what grade you
might have been in, you were sure to punch in those unfamiliar buttons
of "sin," "log," "n!" (and others). Our simple inputs would create mysterious outputs of decimals and *ginormous* numbers. We had no idea
what was going on, but it was fun tooling around with strange functions
if only to see how bizarre our random intentions could be.

Quite often, due to this developing curiosity for math, our answers
would result in an "Error" message. The lack of understanding of the
domain of these advanced buttons was the culprit in us seeing this
perplexing message. Did we do something wrong? Or, as was the case,
was the calculator communicating to us that our answer was not allowed, not plausible, or didn't exist?

As kids, this almost-human message was fun to receive. It's like we
were being gently scolded by our calculator for giving it impossible
tasks. It's really the only time our calculator talked to us. The most common task that led to an irked calculator was the attempt to . . . gulp . . .
take the square root of a negative number.

Square roots of positive numbers are easy peasy: what number mul-
tiplied by itself *exactly* will yield the number asked for? For example,
the square root of 25 is not only +5, but –5 as well. Remember, when

you multiply two negative numbers, the result will be positive. But, Houston, we have a problem. Why did you have to remember this rule? Why didn't you have to, dare I say, *understand it*?

DISCOVERING FROM PLAYING

Nine times 4 is 36. That seems like an odd way to start a paragraph. Is there something peculiar about this equality? No. In fact, it's not the mathematics that is being probed—yet. It's the sentence structure. Oh, grammatically it is fine. It's just that if we reverse the sentence or give it a joyful 180-degree spin, we have opened the sentence to new possibilities.

Thirty-six is 9 times 4.

Did you notice the difference? Do you see the infinite set of answers? Sure, 36 is 9 × 4, but it is also 6 × 6, 12 × 3, 36 + 0, $10^2 - 8^2$, 7 squared minus the sixth prime number, the eighth triangle number, the number of consecutive bowling strikes to bowl three perfect games, and the number of candles lit during Chanukah.

But beyond opening the classroom to greater participation, the tinkering of a standard statement in math opens the door to really understanding why the multiplication of two negative numbers results in a mysterious positive. Seeing multiplication as area gives the explanation some valuable visual aid. Let's start by modeling 9 × 4 as an area question:

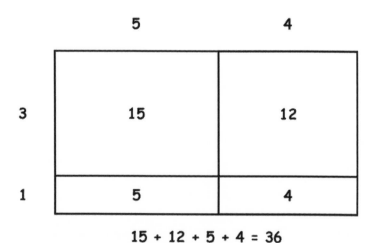

Figure 5.1. *Modeling multiplication with area.*

In figure 5.1, we have taken a playful look at 9×4—and have just randomly partitioned it up, not surprisingly ending up with the same answer of 36! Children these days learn to play with numbers—pulling them apart and putting them back together in creative fashion . . . much like LEGO. Let's continue to *play*—you can never emphasize play enough when talking about math—and add a little twist to our area model:

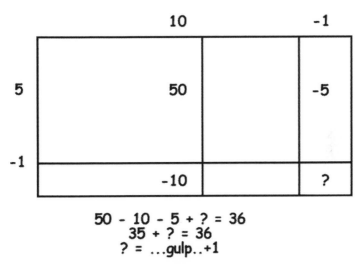

$$50 - 10 - 5 + ? = 36$$
$$35 + ? = 36$$
$$? = ...gulp..+1$$

Figure 5.2.   Mathematical play results in mathematical convention.

Whatever the narrative that you want to use to describe when multiplying with only one negative number, it should have less of a gimmicky answer rooted in memorization. For example, you owe one dollar to 10 people. How much do you owe? The *owing* is what necessitates a negative sign. If the areas that we have so far are added up, we will have $50 + (-10) + (-5)$ gives us 35. Hmmm. We are a "dollar" short! That mystery box must be *positive* one . . . or else the universe and the multiplication of 9×4 will cease to make any sense. (Okay, that was a little dramatic, but that *worried* animation would work well in a primary classroom.)

The convention to adopt the multiplication of two negative numbers now gets fleshed out by that mother of invention—necessity. And, even better, there is a communal and shared adoption of this new rule. It didn't just fall out of the mathematical sky and land in the classroom like some mysterious moon rock. It was a product (ha-ha, get it) of mathematical discovery.

Discovery. Not sure how it happened or when it happened, but one of the most important words in how our whole civilization evolved is used pejoratively by some when associated with learning mathematics. You know . . . *discovery mathematics*. The natural and historical narrative of how math was learned for thousands of years is now somehow a process of learning that is deemed ass-backward, stifling, and confusing.

IT'S A SMALL WORLD AFTER ALL

Personally discovering the secrets, surprises, and idiosyncrasies of math is not only a beneficial way to learn, it's tons of fun. Having mathematics pop out of sterilized packages, precooked and all, is probably unhealthy as well. But, don't take it from me; let's ask the thousands of frustrated math students who exit high school every year. A good 30 percent will join millions who would choose cleaning toilets over doing a math problem. Sigh . . .

Forget appreciating the blade of grass, our society whiffs on whole pastures of Irish green. Gratitude has undergone some inflation over the last few generations. Henry Miller's sweet spot of writing and reflection came in less-processed and frenetic times. We are now in the age of speed and skimming. A blade of grass sadly cannot evoke the philosophical melancholy as much these days. Yet, a blade of grass—almost literally—is what is needed to find mathematical gratitude.

In life, taking things for granted and gratitude have a peculiar dance with each other. What we normally take for granted—health, family, and friends—are the pillars of gratefulness that often only become apparent when they are removed, or reflected upon with a similar sharp clarity that Henry Miller alludes to in the opening quote. Since the essence of this chapter is to find the gratitude in living in the age of cracking the secrets of the stubborn nut of imaginary numbers, then the focus will be on applications that inspire, entertain, or connect us to being happy humans.

Sometimes, though, what should foster tremendous gratitude is all around us, yet invisible, waiting patiently for the right summons. In this case, things like trees, human anatomy and physiology, and meteorological events have had their design and formations encoded with mathematics that was not fully understood until the 20th century. And it is intrinsically linked to the already mentioned classic error that people encountered when playing with their calculators—the square root of a negative number.

When you teach mathematics without a historical foundation and thematic development, you just get a warehouse of rules and facts that don't have any human interjection or inflection. In January 2017, Oxford mathematician and popular blogger Junaid Mubeen wrote a compelling article called "Mathematics without History Is Soulless"—another timely reminder that children need to be told the story of mathematics. I am not sure you get a more gripping tale than one that involves *monsters*!

And when you teach mathematics without its colorful and soulful history, you get all the all-star constants of Euler's ridiculously brilliant formula—$e^{\pi i} + 1 = 0$—rolled out on the assembly line with the

---

My family and I moved into our first house in Canada in 1972. There were some odd items left in the house, which included some dusty books. One of these was a grade 12 mathematics textbook. My memory of my childhood has always been oddly acute, often remembering odd chunks of time with vivid detail. I remember the color of this book, black and tan. I remember finding it on the top shelf of the closet that would become my bedroom.

I remember understanding none of what I read, but still feeling fascinated that the numbers I knew so well—remember, I was a counting champ in grade 1—were knitted with letters of the alphabet and a strange mix of brackets and uppercase notations. One of the final chapters had a letter of an alphabet that I had not seen anywhere in the textbook. It was italicized. It was the letter *i*. That is all that I remember . . .

Ten years later, after that foggy introduction to *i* (the imaginary number) I would study it with things like the complex plane, DeMoivre's Theorem, and alternating currents. Truth be told, I was still in a fog. Being told that the square root of –1 is the ninth letter of the alphabet was just as "good" as being told that multiplying two negative numbers gives you a positive. *Where did I come from* was now frustratingly paired with *where did "i" come from* . . .?

packaging that is cheap and effective. Four of these five constants have their own books. In school, there is just enough time for each to get a clichéd anecdote.

To be fair, there are not a lot of great resources on the evolution of the imaginary number. Dozens upon dozens of mathematicians, going back as early as the first century, had varying intersections and insights as to what an imaginary number might be. Most of them, as soon as they came across a square root with a negative, had a general disdain for them and would almost form a historical tradition of despising any workings in this mathematical black hole.

As fun (*not really*) as solving cubic and quartic equations are, routinely coming across answers in the form $a + bi$, the notation bestowed for complex numbers by Descartes (a and b being the real parts and i being the quirky imaginary part), proved to be too much of a headache for even the most seasoned mathematician.

Only in Napoleonic times did the instinct that imaginary numbers could have any benefit really emerge. Everything would remain relatively in the dark for another century, but for the first time in history, mathematicians were beginning to navigate the landscape of imaginary numbers with growing optimism.

THE NEED FOR IMAGINARY NUMBERS

The first need for imaginary numbers arose in the field of electrical engineering when scientists had to reconcile the differences in direct and alternating currents. In DC circuits, things like voltage, resistance, and current are expressed and work harmoniously as scalar quantities—one dimension only. But, in AC circuits, the above variables produced results that were not the expected scalar ones seen in direct currents. It turned out that these currents—aptly named as alternating—were being influenced by new dimensions like frequency and phase shift. Multidimensional representation was needed to account for all these influencing agents.

Scalar representation was abandoned for the simple reason that they just could not describe the behavior of currents. This requirement of adding another dimension to indicate evolution in understanding has strong parallels to the story line that exists in Edwin Abbott's classic book, *Flatland*, a story of multiple dimensions with a sharp commentary of social hierarchy in Victorian England. Just think of alternating currents as those having the most esteemed position with their multidimensional state and direct currents being lowly one-dimensional entities.

The 19th-century engineer Charles Steinmetz would get credit for using the imaginary number in electricity—the first important application of imaginary numbers. The baton for really blowing the lid off imaginary numbers was being unknowingly passed around this time across the ocean. The brilliant French mathematician Henri Poincare would begin to unlock key doors wide open as to where the imaginary numbers would take us—to the frontier of *chaos theory*.

These doors would have remained locked if not for discovering a *mistake* he found in his analysis of motion involving three objects—think of discovering the *Butterfly Effect* in mathematics! The standard motion between two bodies—let's say the earth and the moon—were studied first by Johann Kepler in the 16th century, and solved in a tidy fashion by Sir Isaac Newton some 80 years later. The notion of introducing a third body made things, let's say, a little bit *chaotic*. Almost all the time, the interactions of three bodies was totally unpredictable. Algebraic formulas could not work. A new unlocked door had been created. Some marvelous world awaited 20th-century mathematicians on the other side.

A NEW WORLD DISORDER

The opposite of chaos is order. And if anything ever described math for the longest time, it was an order of an almost orthodox magnitude. But, if alternating currents hinted at anything, it was that our world is filled with just as much disorder as order. These are not incompatible ideas. If anything, they are sometimes intertwined—complex ideas can emerge from simpler ones; order can come from chaos. And from chaos emerges . . . *life*.

Chaos theory goes through math's *Looking Glass*—the world of imaginary numbers. It doesn't go through it lightly. It's a road trip that would-be mathematics' psychedelic awakening of the 20th century—stretching the imagination with mind-altering explorations and applications. The world that we have inhabited for thousands of years has had its pattering and symmetry soaked in mathematics. This is hardly a revelation. However, the only geometry that had been understood to the world had been the 2,000-year-old Euclidean one.

Unfortunately, only structures of human construction could really live in the world of Euclidean geometry. Perfectly smooth structures like lines and squares and lines of parallel and perpendicular nature exist in the manufactured world—one that is made by humans. Nature's math is literally more complex.

Euclid's *Minecraftish* mathematics would go unchallenged until the Napoleonic times. The world was quite literally thrown a curveball. Interest in straight lines was expiring and being replaced by curiosity of curved surfaces. This was kind of ironic as humans have lived on a curved surface longer than Euclid's postulates—although for a good chunk of time his influential mathematics deemed the world to be similarly flat.

The new ideas were named Riemannian geometry after the 19th-century mathematician Bernhard Riemann. His Riemann Hypothesis is one of the Millennium problems in which the Clay Mathematics Institute offers $1 million to anyone who can prove or disprove it.

It's almost like humans needed a couple millennia to have the resources and resourcefulness to begin not only to deeply contemplate and comprehend the spherical dominance of the universe, but also the mysterious dominance of a *rougher* geometry—fractals. If the history of mathematics could be whimsically compressed into 100 years, fractal geometry just came out last month!

ANOTHER BEAUTIFUL MATH POEM

After the sad passing of the iconic artist David Bowie in January 2016, a powerful—and a correct—meme surfaced that said, "Be thankful you lived in the time of David Bowie." The mathematical equivalence of Bowie's boldness, creativity, and time as an influential artist has strong parallels to fractal geometry. Our physical world. Our languages. Our anatomy. Our physiology. Our creations. Everything owed to fractals. Everything owed to chaos theory. Everything owed to . . . imaginary numbers. *Changes*? Why, yes, indeed . . .

Henry Miller was completely unaware that he was pointing us in the right direction when he called for a close examination of grass, as even the most innocuous gift of nature has fractal connection. If Miller had taken a bird's-eye view of a meadow, perhaps he would have remarked at all the variations of grass blades—depending on their angle to the sun. What he would have missed, like the thousands of mathematicians before him, is that meadow was rich in poetry and math. Alas, math *is* poetry.

> There is nothing as dreamy and poetic, nothing as radical, subversive, and psychedelic, as mathematics.
>
> —Paul Lockhart

Fractals are the poster children for Lockhart's quote. Google images for fractals. They are to math as what David Bowie was to music—revolutionary, colorful, and transcending. They have been encoded in nature since the beginning of time with the ridiculous simplicity of self-similarity—infinite repetition of the same structure at every level. So, whether you zoom in or out, what you see is always the same structure.

In 2017, Florence Williams wrote a beautiful article for the *Atlantic* called "Why Fractals Are So Soothing." The article explored the paintings from the 1950s of the American painter Jackson Pollock. It turned out that Pollock was painting nature's fractals a full quarter of a century before their scientific discovery in 1975. It gets better. Was there something happening in our bodies and brains that was attracting us to these paintings?

Research scientists studied skin conductance and brain waves of people who were watching geometric fractal images. They found measured instances of relaxation and stimulation of brain areas that are involved in pleasurable emotions. Staring at an ocean—its waves are fractals—produced the same effects as listening to calming classical music! One of the research scientists, Richard Taylor, believes that our brains are wired to have a kinship with nature—mathematics literally making us happy!

And while these fractal structures are infinitely complex, the infinite loop they are trapped in always produces shapes/designs that are bounded—finite. It is infinity and finiteness existing in geometric harmony. It is no small wonder why it took so long for fractals to be discovered. The best things in life are worth waiting for. Be grateful that you existed in the time of Bowie and . . . *Benoit*!

MONSTER INC.

Benoit Mandelbrot is the father of fractals, a fact that is almost part of pop culture, thanks to the hundreds of trippy Mandelbrot zoom videos on YouTube, many set to pulsating trance music. The level of zooming—magnification—has now surpassed the number of hydrogen atoms in the observable universe.

A closer number for understanding the sheer absurdity and audacity of his magnification involves stuffing as many Plank spaces—about one septillion times smaller than a hydrogen atom—into the observable universe. Who would have thought that *error* on the calculator would become a mathematical hallucinogen? Square roots of negative numbers. The *gateway* math . . .

One thing I do to bring happiness and community to mathematics is participate in Family Math Nights. Think of them as fun evening math fairs with refreshments. One of the most popular stations is "LEGO Broccoli." Here kids use only the square pieces of LEGO (green) and build these strange-looking pyramids. The broccoli reference is to the beautiful Romanesco broccoli that has vivid fractals.

This structure can be replicated with just four of those square LEGO pieces, attaching them in a way to make a blockish-looking pyramid. Then kids and parents take four of these mini pyramids and build a larger one that looks the same. Then we take four of these and build a level 3 pyramid. And so on. The "so on" is the hook: 256 pieces of LEGO later, we've built a stunning level 4 Sierpinski pyramid.

They came for the free food, but they stayed for the math . . .

Even though Mandelbrot's ideas about fractals had come to the forefront by the 1970s, his seminal work, *Form, Chance and Dimension,* would help harvest one of the first applications of fractals. It would be at least another decade before collective excitement would come. But once it did, the floodgates opened. Areas of study including—but not limited to—engineering, electronics, chemistry, human physiology, medicine, economics, urban planning, film, and public policy began to flourish.

Fractal applications are varied and seem to be growing every day, and yet they are housed in such a quirky and literally irregular branch of mathematics. This is kind of fitting. You see, the brilliance of Mandelbrot was a function of some serious irregularities in his upbringing. War, poverty, and basic survival kept him out of conventional education in his high school years. He even credited much of his successful insights to his extraordinary circumstances, and the atypical learning that had to ensue. Much of his creativity must have been welded in adversity. His education was the farthest thing from . . . *inert*. His aim was about as true as it gets.

THE 370-MILLION-YEAR-OLD SECRET EXPOSED

Trees have been around for a good long time. Often called the lungs of the earth, trees are crucial Earth partners in our own breathing process. Trees produce oxygen, which keeps our lungs alive, which keeps us alive. It's a simple relationship. But, it is also a strong one, thanks to fractals. Look at a tree. Trunk, branches, and twigs. Look at our lungs. Trachea, bronchi, and bronchioles. The structural identity is rooted in the self-similarity of fractals. This ideal configuration yields the most efficient way to help produce oxygen in a limited, finite space. Our grand design is complex—physically and mathematically. Who could have ever imagined it? Benoit Mandelbrot. That's who!

While the comprehension of Mandelbrot's rough universe was in its infancy to mathematicians 50 years ago, today its understanding is both broad and deep—as the mining for new applications continues intensively. Whole books are now available detailing all the varied applications. One of the best in terms of being contemporary in approach and accessibility is *Fractals: A Graphic Guide* (2014). Having the feel of a retro comic strip, the book does an excellent job of both cool storytelling and explaining the mathematics behind fractals.

TO BOLDLY GO

Going to the movies has been a time-honored tradition for many generations. The theatergoing experience for some movies is enhanced by the uncanny realism of backgrounds, terrains, and landscapes. You can thank fractals for creating these scenes that are so real that they can sometimes not be distinguished from the actual images.

The first movie to explore this new technology was the 1982 movie *Star Trek II: The Wrath of Khan.* A fractal-generated landscape was created in the movie. Not too ironic is the fact that land formations and mountains exhibit fractal behavior of self-similarity. Another case of math helping art imitating life.

Before we move forward with the applications of fractals, I need to mention the wonderful work Dr. Ron Eglash has done in illuminating the indigenous fractal design in many African societies. A wonderful TED Talk and a book by him are now available detailing how a good portion of Africa had been using fractals in the design of clothing, housing, and tribal customs before Mandelbrot's discoveries were published in the West. The fact that we already know the natural existence of fractals, the notion that ancient societies might see the cultural and aesthetic benefits of fractals before a formal mathematical explanation shouldn't be the least bit surprising.

In the late 1990s, McDougal Littell released the textbook *Algebra II: Explorations and Applications.* The book included a section titled "Sequences and Series: Fractals for Fashions" due to mathematicians discovering the technologically savvy fashion designer Jhane Barnes. Her textile innovations were rich and extensive, full of intricacies that reflected the fractal world that had been unfolding for over a decade now. Never thinking of herself as a "math person," she admitted her weakness for math in the best fractal documentary ever made, PBS Nova's *Fractals: Hunting the Hidden Dimension.*

It is a one-hour documentary that not only captures the mathematics of a fractal, more importantly, it captures seasoned mathematicians wanting to share their insights with excitement, joy, and wonder. The versatility of fractals is one of the most marvelous aspects of them. At one moment, they are the artistic inspiration of a self-confessed *mathphobe* and, in another instance, they are embedded in ancient customs of tribes in Africa. And then, there are those moments of mathematical serendipity that are catalysts for historical breakthroughs.

Nathan Cohen, a Boston radio astronomer, had the fortunate opportunity to hear Mandelbrot talk about the large-scale structure of the universe and how fractals could help play a role in understanding that. Cohen also happened to have a hobby tinkering with ham radios. All these elements played a part in Cohen experimenting with traditional antennas and fashioning them into more efficient and compact spaces. He started to bend wires.

His initial wire figures paid homage to the Koch Snowflake, one of the first fractal curves to be described. Eventually, he would fashion a square antenna that rotated 45 degrees and looked sort of like a Celtic cross. The significance of this compact antenna was that not only did it conserve space, but allowed for a wider range of frequencies to be received. Without this invention, an antenna to have this strength and frequency range would stick out six feet and have rather grotesque tentacles (needed to capture all the different frequencies).

Without Nathan Cohen, Benoit Mandelbrot, and the dimension expansion of the square root of a negative number—these combining forces of creativity and imagination—there would be no cell phones. No cell phones? That is correct. All those students lamenting about the crappiness of their math classes through texts and tweets—quite often while they're still in their math classes—would be served well with a gentle reminder of this not so teeny-weeny application.

FRACTALS ARE EVERYWHERE

Keeping track of all the beneficial applications of mathematics for society is truly a thankless job. Every day each one of us receives benefits of research in medicine, technology, science, engineering, nutrition, psychology, and other areas. And there isn't a cue forming any time soon to show gratitude for living in a society with such advances. That is why as amazing mathematics is enhancing our lifestyle, it is far more important for it to enhance the simplicities in our life—purchasing and moving faster must yield to *pondering and slowing down*.

Fractals are stunning mathematics creations that are, quite frankly, dizzying. Roping in infinity after a dreary sojourn of historical dismissal, the Ugly Duckling of mathematics is now as regal as they come. Yes, the applications continue to be groundbreaking. For example, a healthy heartbeat has an irregular fractal heartbeat that apes the jaggedness of mountains. Further research here might develop markers to identify early heart diseases.

Even cancer research is investigating how healthy blood flow in an organ—like the bifurcations of a tree—differs from the vasculature of a tumor. The goal is to see if early detection of cancers can be spotted with microscopic alterations in otherwise healthy fractal blood flow.

That all said, the sale of mathematics must be negotiated on more personal and magical terms. In Dr. Eglash's groundbreaking TED Talk in 2007, the opening remarks cut right to the chase—Georg Cantor. The story of where infinity takes off is the story of where fractal discussions begin. Eglash is clever enough to recognize this and gives Cantor his due by wasting no time with any preamble about himself or anything else.

In the next few minutes, he focuses on the disgruntlement that these fractal curves caused mathematicians of the day. These were the monsters that emanated from Cantor sets. For Eglash, these were "pathological" curves of the day—having little use and relegated to the back of textbooks. Just a few moments later, not only does he prove the humanness of fractals, he does so in a way that is powerfully endearing.

He lifts his right hand up in the air, focusing on the slack region between the thumb and the index finger. He points to this flappy skin and remarks that there are wrinkles here that have crinkles, and those crinkles have wrinkles . . . and so on. It's an unintended moment of intense transmission of teaching and connection. You could almost imagine him sitting down in a kindergarten classroom doing the same activity, asking children to poke around in their own playground of mathematics.

Shouldn't we be teaching fractals in schools? Shouldn't we be teaching fractals in schools at an *early age*? Our bodies, externally and internally, are covered with fractals. The fact that the mathematics is beyond most of the requirements of school is a *blessing*, not a curse. It means not everything will be revealed just yet. It means that students will have to pursue mathematics at a higher level to truly understand the captivating details of fractals and imaginary numbers.

Fractals. The simplicity of self-similarity. The crossing of paths with infinity. The courage of its discoverer. Do you see how mathematics is not sterile or inert? It goes beyond intersecting our lives. It is our lives. Our breath, our blood flow, and our small patch of skin on our hands—our very own *blade of grass* to moon over.

Just rewind the tape back to when our calculators *spoke* to us about the impossibility of our harmless input—what is the square root of a negative number. In your wildest imaginations, could you have conjured the vivid landscape that lay beyond the calculator wall? Most likely not. The element of surprise and wonder has always been a calling card for mathematics. But surprise and wonder are universal markers for happiness.

That's life—where the small idiosyncrasies of mathematics are often its greatest treasures. But the story of imaginary numbers has been one strange tale. From disdain and disregard to delight and discovery. Often, we talk about treasuring life's smaller moments. Isn't this the core idea of a fractal—a beautiful idea replicated at smaller and smaller levels? Aren't our lives physically—and *philosophically*—fractals? The square root of a negative number literally symbolizes the gratitude that lies in wait for all of us—sometimes hidden, but always available.

CHAPTER 6

Seventeen

Health

The brain is wider than the sky.

—Emily Dickinson

There have been many studies over the past few years that have shown that elderly people who participate in daily mental activities, such as word games or puzzles, demonstrate a marked acuity in daily activities like grocery shopping and managing finances. Intuitively this shouldn't be surprising to anyone. Being immersed in any kind of logical problem solving necessitates richer blood flow to the participating regions of the brain. As well, synapses and axons are continually firing off. Mental gymnastics is literally and figuratively the workout gym for the brain.

The biggest puzzle craze of this century has been Sudoku. Introduced to the West by the *Times* of London in 2004, Sudoku took off immediately. In a few short years, over 140 newspapers around the world would carry daily Sudoku puzzles. Some might even argue that certain newspapers staved off impending extinction due to frenzied demand of this box puzzle. The legion of millions who became devotees of this number puzzle included the strangest bedfellows—those who loved math and those who hated math.

For the math aficionados, Sudoku was just one more puzzle to be tackled in probably a long menu of puzzles that included cryptic crosswords, logic puzzles, brain teasers, and various other math entanglements. For the bemoaning math folks, Sudoku might have been the first real intersection of numbers *and* fun. Up until then, root canals were the popular response to "I'd rather have a _____ than do math."

Despite some of the key hallmarks of mathematical thinking employed in cracking Sudoku puzzles—strategy and patience—many members of the anti-math community would scoff at the idea that this was . . . *math*. No. It wasn't some of the scrambled alphabet soup that accompanied the polynomials and algebra found in schools, but if the actual gameplay was possibly divorced from math, its construction was most certainly not.

Most people who play Sudoku got their first introduction in newspapers. And as newspapers are written for mass circulation, the clear majority of the puzzles found here tend to be of average difficulty. You need some sleuthing sharps, but usually a subway ride to work will be sufficient time to crack the Sudokus found in the puzzle section of newspapers.

A standard Sudoku grid has 9 squares with 9 cells each for a total of 81 cells. The familiar goal of Sudoku is to obey the *one rule* and place the numbers 1 to 9 only once in each row and column of the grid. As well, for a further constraint, each of the 9 mini-squares must also contain every number from 1 to 9. What makes a Sudoku puzzle unique is that it is *unique*. Every Sudoku puzzle has only one solution. Imagine a blank Sudoku grid and you had to fill the numbers in such a way that this one rule was obeyed. There would be more than one way to fill these 81 squares in. To be specific, around 670 quintillion.

The point is to have a unique solution so there is no other way to complete the grid. Most newspapers had puzzles that started with 25 numbers filled in. Eventually, as the popularity grew, people began to wonder what was the fewest number of starting clues to create a unique solution. It didn't take long before the mythical number of 16 started to percolate in Sudoku circles. Unique solutions with 17 had already been found, but in the style of that 1970s game show *Name That Tune*, puzzle fans wanted to solve that puzzle with the fewest "notes" possible.

None would be found. The collective instincts of the *Sudokuphiles* soon would give rise to the strong notion that unique Sudokus were not available with 16 clues. The magic number for the fewest number of starting clues seemed to be stalled on 17. Gut instincts—even a million of them—as you know by now have little currency in the mathematical world. Proof or go home is the gold standard.

HUMAN CREATIVITY CREATES COMPUTER SHORTCUT

Gary McGuire, a mathematician at the University College Dublin, ran with that adage as his computers worked for a solid year until it was verified that no Sudoku with 16 starting clues has a unique solution. That is *not* the amazing part. The amazing part was samurai-slicing of the problem by the *human*, Gary McGuire. The mathematical analysis that preceded the computer analysis was the masterstroke. Without it, computers would have needed 300,000 years to check all the required grids. By that time, they would have figured out how to unionize themselves, don't you think!?

So, what happened? What kind of insights allowed for the answer to this Sudoku mystery to be unraveled in a calendar year?

Mathematicians are pattern searchers who love symmetry. It turns out that the number of actual Sudoku grids that need analysis can be drastically reduced by transposing and rotating grids. In the sharp and tidy Numberphile video on this breakthrough, the wide-eyed, alacritous host James Grime explains how the number of 16-clue Sudoku grids can be reduced from 330 quadrillion to a paltry five billion.

However, an odd, mildly self-deprecating comment is asked off-camera by the show's video maker, Brady Haran—"surely there are better things to do with your time." This is not the first time Haran has played the devil's advocate in these "math love" videos. However, here the purposeful scripting is designed to funnel the exhaustive proof by McGuire into potential future applications—some that might benefit the public. That is all fine and dandy, but the apologist tone that this video ends up getting framed in was not only unnecessary, it was short-sighted.

The results in math have always had center stage. Well, in all discoveries really. One of the reasons is this subconscious nod to "how can this benefit me?" This is a valid question, but there seems to be often this sterile decapitation of the *findings* from the *finder*. Sure, there is some accompanying bio information that gets woven into the story, but it's more of a chopped up and pureed LinkedIn profile. The best part of these stories—the human narrative of wonder—often drowns in the headlines. When people relay travel stories, our interest should not just be where they went, but *why* they went there . . . and of course, *who* went there!

This is what happened to Gary McGuire. But, in mathematics especially, there seems to be this need to justify the hundreds of hours of research, which unjustly waffles near the Brady Haran cynicism. Again, that skeptical eye is part of the production/branding of some of the Numberphile videos. It creates dialogue that might be found quite easily in everyday conversation, which is why Numberphile is so popular.

Numberphile explores and unpacks quirky or complex mathematical ideas with narration that is whimsical and casual, purposely aiming to go beyond the math communities. When Matt Parker is explaining number theory on a table in a mall (instead of a university lecture hall), you know that he wants to look at the seriousness of math in ways that are *anything but* serious.

So, what did the fine folks at Numberphile miss? They missed what many have glossed over—the happiness of mathematics.

> The best moments in our lives are not the passive, receptive, relaxing times. . . . The best moments usually occur if a person's body or mind is stretched to its limits in a voluntary effort to accomplish something difficult and worthwhile.
>
> —Mihaly Csikszentmihalyi

GO WITH THE FLOW

In Mihaly Csikszentmihalyi's book *Flow: The Psychology of Optimal Experience*, universal conditions for "flow" are outlined. In a truncated examination of this idea, his 2008 TED Talk also discussed these markers for people being in this effusive state. In his talk, he mentions that he surveyed 8,000 people. To underscore how these conditions for happiness were truly global and disconnected from things like culture, education, and income, he interviewed people like Dominican monks, blind nuns, and Navajo shepherds.

Below are the criteria for flow that Csikszentmihalyi's research discovered. As you look at them, not only reflect on Gary McGuire, but more important, reflect on yourself:

- Completely involved in what we are doing—focused and concentrated.
- A sense of ecstasy—of being outside everyday reality.
- Great inner clarity—know what needs to get done, and how well we are doing.
- Knowing that the activity is doable—that our skills are adequate to the task.
- A sense of serenity—no worries about oneself, and a feeling of growing beyond the boundaries of the ego.
- Timelessness—thoroughly focused on the present, hours seem to pass by as minutes.
- Intrinsic motivation—whatever produces flow becomes its own reward.

We don't have to go too far down the list to realize that Gary McGuire was in flow. The notion about future applications was never on his radar. He was in the moment. He was deep in optimal experience. If Kafka were alive, he might be less vague with the quote that is found at the end of the introduction to this book. Summon it by the right word? That word would be *flow* . . .

McGuire's Sudoku proof was definitely flow. But what about actually *doing* a Sudoku? Could we get caught in a similar current of euphoria? Absolutely.

Everything stems from the brain. Look at people who have diseases like Alzheimer's. Their body is fine, but the brain function has all but disappeared. Sadly, the body shortly follows suit. Then look at the opposite case—people whose bodies have completely withered, but their minds are in pristine shape. Many people who are diagnosed with ALS or Lou Gehrig's disease pass away within five years of diagnosis. Then there's Stephen Hawking, who at the time this book was written, is living fully at the age of 74.

Diagnosed when he was 21, Hawking has a variant of ALS that progresses slowly. That said, there must be something happening at the epicenter of his thoughts/discoveries that has prolonged his life. Has the intensity of his mathematical insights to the structure of the universe played a role in his happiness? Yes. Does happiness prolong life? It would be challenging to answer that question without data—whatever that data even looks like. This much is true: happiness should be the goal in life that we want for ourselves and others.

If there was a single mathematician who has been responsible for trying to flesh out the joy of problem solving, it has to be Martin Gardner, who we were fortunate to have with us for almost 100 years. He died at the age of 96 back in 2010. Martin Gardner wrote over 60 books. That's a lot of time popularizing mathematics! But, what was Gardner doing that made his presentation of math so lively and buoyant (and so popular)? Well, for one, he wasn't finding the heights of kites or factoring polynomials in his problems.

Surveying the titles of Gardner's library, we come across titles like *Mathematics: Magic and Mystery*; *The Annotated Alice*; *Codes, Ciphers and Secret Writing*; *Aha! Gotcha*; *Origami, Eleusis and the Soma Cube*; *Gardner's Whys and Wherefores*; *Knotted Doughnuts and Other Mathematical Entertainments; Mathematical Carnival*, among others.

Etcetera. It just goes on. If Willy Wonka was a mathematician, he would have been Martin Gardner. But instead of just writing books, he would have also opened up a museum that had demonstrations, illusions, illuminations, and exaltations that screamed the magic of mathematics. Unbridled with no compromise, a mathematical Wonka would have turned mathematics into a Fourth of July fireworks display meets Halloween in an amusement park. Complete sensory overload. A modern version of all that is wondrous, whimsical, and wacky in math now exists in New York City's *Museum of Mathematics*, a lovely 19,000 square-foot facility in Manhattan that opened in December 2012.

Gardner's success was due to finding the absolute best puzzles and problems. Questions that intrigued us, mystified us, and stupefied us. The hook was in the question. His problems were baited with simplicity, intuition, and intrinsic wonder. He took us *slantways*. His mathematics was quite often prefaced with the word *recreational*. It was appropriate in that all his ideas and problems were to be viewed with lighthearted exploration and fun. At the same time, however, this adjective saddled his mathematics with being somehow less than academic, less rigorous . . . less mathematical. Fun and math? Isn't that like oil and water?

I taught mathematics and physics for 19 years. It was nice going out in my "prime." I taught in a challenging inner-city school. I taught in an International Baccalaureate in Switzerland. I taught at a community college. I taught a gifted physics class. I taught solely remedial math classes one year. The common element that linked these was the universal interest to always want a "Mr. Singh" puzzle or brainteaser. Even the students with the most disdainful views of mathematics would spend hours on these problems. After almost 20 years of doing this, I concluded something that was more of an affirmation: kids don't hate math because it's hard; kids hate math because it's boring.

In the following pages, I'll share some of my most popular puzzles, puzzles that crossed not only class and culture boundaries, but also grade levels and academic success. They tapped into universal qualities of curiosity and flow. They were reminders of why mathematics has been globally pursued for thousands of years—for simple joy. There are many problems that can be shared here that are tough nuts to crack, but the all-time favorite for having a colorful history of struggle, frustration, and insanity has to be the 24 Problem.

A quick examination of the words to describe what this puzzle did to students might be seen as negative conditions for learning. But, beyond being prerequisites for being students of math (okay, maybe not the tongue-in-cheek reference to insanity), they serve as the foundation of what is the most desired skill for doing all math—patience.

In 2010, Dan Meyer gave a groundbreaking TED Talk called "Math Class Needs a Makeover." It not only started to steer the conversation toward an almost forensic analysis of math education's misfiring of student engagement, but it launched him into the stratosphere of respected voices on 21st-century learning. Dan Meyer is the rock star of math education. (He is also its first.)

There are lots of pearls of wisdom in Meyer's talk, which sometimes gets overshadowed by his comical commentary on why the classroom needs a makeover. No punches are pulled. And the blows are strongest when addressing textbook problems that were *not* really problems—they were more like *Finding Waldo* questions. How do you do this question? Don't know. Find a similar problem in the "Examples" section, locate the missing pieces of information, and insert them into formulas of zero intuition. Voila! You are now on your way to being anything but a mathematician.

Doing math problems that are more like following a recipe gives not only a false sense of understanding, but it doesn't train the mind for patient problem solving. Some of the most famous math problems took centuries to solve from the brightest people in the history of math. Patience is everything. Imagine if all people were given egg timers to solve math problems. We would all be living in Bedrock driving cars with our feet. Dan Meyer was even more specific. He said that students need to *build patience for irresolution*.

Let that sink in for a bit.

An accomplished math student is one who, ironically, can persevere without accomplishment. Correct answers? *Pffft*. Unless the answer can continue the conversation of the problem or general ideas found therein, correct answers are more like the denouement of a book. The plot of problem solving is the process. The crises are the wrong turns. The heroic climax is finding the most challenging piece of the puzzle. The actual written answer is a mere tidying up of events. Understanding will lead to correctness; correctness will rarely lead to understanding.

Answers that deserve to be in the spotlight are zero, imaginary, infinity, undefined, or some number with real applicable bite. Asking, for example, "where do two lines meet?" is a good exercise for students to work on their algebra skills—manipulating equations with various techniques to eventually isolate one of the two x or y variables to get half the story of the coordinates where these lines intersect. Students will often get these questions wrong because of the many natural places to make mistakes. They will take a peek at the answer at the back of the textbook and groan if their answer is wrong. They will think they don't understand solving equations. They will think they are dumb.

This is what focusing on the least important part of mathematics does—undermines student confidence and undermines mathematics. The journey of inquiry into *interesting* problems is the real narrative of mathematics that truly matters. The flash resolution at the end of these lovable conundrums hopefully only provides interest and motivation for the next round of perplexity.

THE 24 PROBLEM

Put the numbers 1 to 24 down the left-hand side of a piece of paper. On the top, put the numbers 1, 3, 4, and 6. Underneath these key numbers put the operations of +, −, ×, and ÷. The task is to create questions that give the answers for all the numbers from 1 to 24. There are no restrictions on the operations (you can use whichever ones you want as often as you need them). However, you must use each of the numbers 1, 3, 4, and 6 exactly once. And, there can be no concatenation—i.e., you can't construct a "13" by putting the 1 and 3 together.

Here are some of the answers for the first few numbers.

$$1 = (6 - 3) \div (4 - 1)$$
$$2 = (3 + 1) \div (6 - 4)$$
$$3 = (6 - 4 - 1) \times 3$$
$$4 = 6 + 3 - 4 - 1$$

As you can see, some answers will be easier than others.

Fourteen is the easiest: $1 + 3 + 4 + 6$. All the answers are possible. *All of them.* A very strange thing will happen once most people get to 24. Most will get stuck. They will even start to violate the rules—$6 \times 4 \times 1$ is 24, but there is an omission of the 3. Exponents will be desperately and incorrectly brought in like ringers for a baseball beer league. There will be relentless mumbling that this question is impossible. There will be visible frustration and heavy sighing. There will also be *nobody* who wants the answer . . .

I gave the "24 Problem" out to every class I taught in the first week of classes. Every class was told that if all 24 answers to this reverse PEDMAS problem were solved in the time allotted for class (usually 60 minutes), I would purchase pizza for the whole class the coming Friday. In my entire teaching career, I never had to buy a pizza . . .

Almost every class would collectively get the answers from 1 to 23 within 20 to 30 minutes. Confidence would be brimming at this point. Cocky requests for me to throw in a case of soda would sometimes occur. But the last 10 minutes would see panic as though they were on the *Titanic*.

The 24 puzzle works for many reasons. It is in the wheelhouse of where skills meet challenge—the discussed prerequisite for flow. It also creates a huge bounty of success, as the first 23 numbers are obtained with ease and understanding. The "we've come this far and we cannot turn back" mentality is pretty much installed at this point. There is hardly any mathematical mutiny. And yet, victory is rarely found. Remember, the destination of mathematics has always been the journey.

For almost two decades this puzzle has been doled out with the same sheepish introductions. The pizza companies and soda manufacturers changed in the never-obtained rewards, but the stories of hilarious immersion of people into this ostensibly innocent arithmetic problem did not. The funniest story was not about a student. It was about a teacher.

In December 2005, while I was teaching at the International School of Lausanne, I completed my International Baccalaureate training in the beautiful city of Vienna. A city that became even more glowing—literally—with the abundance of many Christmas markets. After the first day of rigorous workshops on how to grade IB papers, I was wiped out. Spending hours meticulously marking these global math exams was gruelling.

I was looking forward to dinner, beers, and conversations about anything but math. At dinner, I was seated near the end of the table. Everyone was seated to the right of me except for this Russian teacher. The conversation that was happening in that direction revolved around travel and being a citizen of the world. I wanted to participate wholly in that discussion, but my Russian friend kept mentally jabbing me with math stuff. It was interesting and all, but I was tapped out with anything to do with numbers.

I then gave him my 24 Problem. I wrote it on a napkin. I figured it would buy me 30 minutes of being "mathless." After the first few minutes of clarification about the rules, silence finally fell. The baby went down for his nap, so to speak. What I didn't know at the time is that this would induce a full-on slumber. He would not only spend half an hour on the problem, he would spend the *whole night* trying to arrange 1, 3, 4, and 6 into a question to give an answer of 24.

At breakfast, looking like he was auditioning for the next *Hangover* movie, he begged for the answer. Grabbing another napkin, I wrote it down. A hearty laugh and a slap on my back were followed by "Dat eez good problem."

In September 2015, the 24 puzzle would find its way into the *New York Times*. They even included the reference to the pizza prize! While none of the other puzzles described below would ever garner such a colorful history of anecdotes and media fame, they would all have their own little stories of devious delight. Student upon student would inadvertently end up in Csikszentmihalyi's stream of happiness—flow.

Just minutes earlier they could have been wallowing in some stagnant pond of purposeless mathematics, only soon to be fully vested in the conditions for optimal experience. Flow is a universal philosophy for happiness. It turns out that even the most resistant student to the charms of mathematics can fall into these currents—with a little push from Gardner.

THE REST OF THE MAGNIFICENT SEVEN

Math puzzles come in all shapes and sizes. Some are number puzzles. Some are visual puzzles. Some are logic puzzles. The key to the best puzzles—and even the best math questions—is that they are clear, compact, and compelling. Wading through lots of text and instructions can sometimes make interesting questions less attractive. Stun the audience with puzzles that perplex with an economy of words. Here are the rest of the Magnificent Seven!

Puzzle Two: Two Kinds of Twist

$$76 = 24$$

In this puzzle, you must rearrange the four numbers so that both sides are equal to each other—it's the only way the equal sign makes sense! Think of the five objects as "fridge magnets," with the equal sign staying fixed and no other magnets allowed. There will be some natural apprehension as there are no operators to work with, and yet, somehow the numbers can be manipulated to show equality.

Puzzle Three: The Disappearing Square

Move only two toothpicks in figure 6.1 so that the configuration goes from five squares of the same size to four squares of the same size.

No overlapping or strange dangling of toothpicks. A counterintuitive problem of not destroying matter (throwing away toothpicks), yet destroying one square!

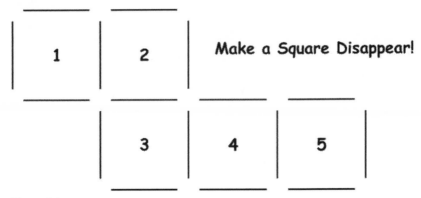

Figure 6.1.

Puzzle Four: The Setup

This one is nasty. It's a combination puzzle, where the answer to the first one has the strong potential to steer many in the wrong direction for the second. In each case, you must draw one straight line left of the equal sign to make each statement true. You will notice there are no operations in the second equation. Reminder: only one straight line!

$$5 + 5 + 5 = 550$$
$$20 \quad 10 \quad 5 \quad = 440$$

Puzzle Five: The Almost Impossible Crossing

There are three guards (GGG) and three prisoners (Ppp). There is a motorboat in which all the guards and only one prisoner know how to operate. All six people are on one side of the lake. All six people must end up at the other side of the lake. The rules are that the boat can only accommodate two people and at no time can prisoners outnumber guards—that includes being on the boat (so, for example, a boat with a guard and a prisoner arriving to a side that contains only a prisoner would mean the guard is outnumbered). The boat can obviously go back and forth. Just be mindful that only one of the prisoners can drive the boat. (This problem is a great exercise in patience and persistence.)

Puzzle Seven: Hunters and Rabbits

This goal of this puzzle is to place five hunters (H) and three rabbits (R) in the grid below so that no rabbit is in the line of fire of any hunter. Hunters can shoot forward, backward, vertically, horizontally, and diagonally. For the purposes of this puzzle, it is quite all right for a hunter to be in the line of sight of another hunter. Figure 6.2 shows that placing just four hunters in this configuration allows *not even one* rabbit to be safe!

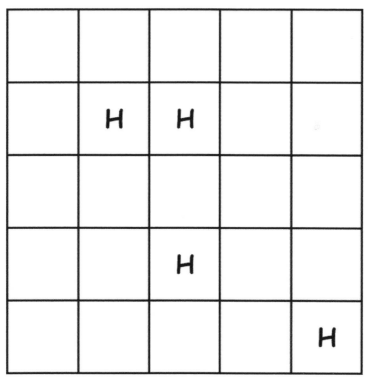

Figure 6.2.

Puzzle Seven: To Cross the Bridge

There are four people. For the sake of clarity, let's call them *A*, *B*, *C*, and *D*. It takes them 10, 5, 2, and 1 minute(s), respectively, to cross this bridge. Given the following conditions, what is the fastest time for all four people to cross the bridge?

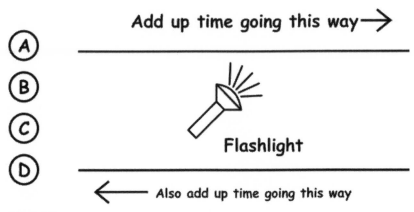

Figure 6.3.

- Only one or two people can cross the bridge at one time.
- There is one flashlight. It must always be carried crossing the bridge.
- When two people walk together, they walk at the speed of the slower one.

So if *A* and *C* cross the bridge, it will take 10 minutes. *C*, being the faster person, should walk back with the flashlight to any remaining members.

So a total of 12 minutes of walking time is used with the *A*/*C* pairing.

Nineteen minutes is *not* the answer. It's the answer most people get. The answer is faster than that!

CLIMBING MOUNTAINS AND MATH

Hopefully you found lots of pleasure in exercising your brain. Most of these problems might have been encountered for the first time. Hopefully you managed to have some insights, breakthroughs, and epiphanies. But, more than that, you became engaged and happy with your persistence and the problem at hand. The reason to study mathematics is mathematics itself.

There is a whole universe of puzzles that Martin Gardner helped create. You would need several books just to list all the books and resources on puzzles and brainteasers. This is ample evidence that millions of people are scaling the hills and mountains of mathematical thinking. They are all tapping into finding moments where they can be lost in the wilderness of their contemplation, far from the civilization of duty and obligation.

> The mystique of rock climbing is climbing; you get to the top of a rock glad it's over but really wish it would go on forever. The justification of climbing is climbing, like the justification of poetry is writing; you don't conquer anything except things in yourself. . . . The act of writing justifies poetry. Climbing is the same: recognizing that you are a flow. The purpose of the flow is to keep on flowing, not looking for a peak or utopia but staying in the flow. It is not a moving up but a continuous flowing; you move up to keep the flow going. There is no possible reason for climbing except the climbing itself; it is a self-communication.
>
> —Mihaly Csikszentmihalyi

Doing math for fun is beneficial for keeping our minds sharp and active. While doing so, we are also experiencing flow, the psychological explanation of happiness. However, when we take a serious look at it, there are some hidden real-life applications to be found. Lighthearted excursions in math give us happy moments in life; the stern examinations in math give us power and control. Grab your cape—it's time to fly!

CHAPTER 7

ME

Power

Probability is the very guide of life.

—Cicero

Hold your breath. Count to three. Come with me. Do you recognize these words? Hopefully you do. Their resonance goes far and deep with me. Those are the words said by Willy Wonka in the 1971 movie *Willy Wonka and the Chocolate Factory*. The words are infused with power as they are said in the scene when the kids and the adults in the film see inside the chocolate factory for the first time. It's pure magic. It's pure imagination.

> There is no world I know like pure imagination. Living there you will be free if you truly wish to be.
>
> —Willy Wonka

It is one of the best visual metaphors for what mathematics is—a trippy dream state of boundless creativity and freedom. The first scene of the movie that was shot was the lengthy dash of an exuberant Charlie after he quite unexpectedly finds the last *Golden Ticket*. Lance Fortnow's delectable book, *The Golden Ticket: P, NP and the Search for the Impossible*, is a direct reference to obtaining the keys to a currently fictitious mathematical kingdom—that would be the equivalent of the *Chocolate Factory*. It's a mind-blowing read of the famous computer science problem about whether all problems that can be verified by a computer for being correct can be solved by a computer.

Checking is the easy part for a computer. Asking it to solve a problem can often go beyond the boundaries and time of a computer. Just look back at some of the human work that Gary McGuire did before he assigned his computers to find a solution. He turned the potential marathon of work into a relative sprint.

Take an innocent problem like this one: supposing you want to take all your harvested pumpkins to market. Let's say you have 200 pumpkins. They all have different masses. You are going to crate them into boxes. Each box can only hold 50 pounds without breaking. Will 12 boxes be enough? What the computer will do here is try all the millions of combinations at lightning speed. It's doing the same brute force calculations we would do, it's just trying to do them faster.

Sigh. Even the rocket velocity of a computer can be useless at times. Going to the moon at 25,000 mph might be a fun thing to do on a Saturday afternoon—a nice 10-hour jaunt in outer space. Going at that speed to even our nearest star, Alpha Centauri, would involve a magnitude of time that has no practicality for humans. This same analogy applies to computers. Are we excited about our fastest computer cranking out the solution in 300,000 years? I think not.

While that all might sound overwhelming and disempowering, there is a mathematical concept that all of us can wield mightily and practically. It's not a faster way of doing taxes or making your carpentry skills sharper. It's about a simple formula—a *very simple* formula—that can save you money. It's the same formula that makes billions for certain corporations.

MATHEMATICAL EXPECTATION

Tom Henderson, a renegade mathematician from Portland, has a catchphrase on his website that epitomizes the punk ethos of wielding the sword of mathematics—"learn math, do more damage." The damage he refers to is against corporations that prey upon the mathematical illiteracy of the general population.

Expectation is a word commonly used by all of us. It can mean a belief about the future from meteorological conditions to economic trends to even just adherence to social norms. It is also associated with anticipation or confidence in personal fulfillment. Regardless of the usage, we *always understand* what these expectations are and the reasons behind them. If you Google *expectation*, the first bulleted definitions of any result will refer to the above familiar situations.

But there is an expectation that suffers from a low billing and never cracks the top three definitions. It is called *Mathematical Expectation*, and it is the one expectation that you desperately need to understand—but probably do not.

Now don't go rummaging through the contents of the mental attic of the high school math that you once learned. You will not find it under the rubble of polynomials, angle bisectors, and cosines. And, unless you had some renegade math teacher, this might even be the first time you have even heard of this expression. However, history is on your side. Shrouded with an off-putting numerical veil, mathematical expectation has remained hidden from the public for its entire existence.

Its anonymity—purposeful some might say—is the economic engine for insurance companies, casinos, warranty providers, and government lotteries. Our collective failure to understand mathematics is symbolized by our ignorance of this concept, and how effortlessly it siphons billions of dollars out of all our pockets every year.

The Secret? Two hundred glossy pages with an embossed cover that was, in the end, one Deepak Chopra riff slowed down and repeatedly played for the unconscious collective. Mathematical Expectation (ME), on the other hand, is the *real* secret, and its unlocking should have occurred in your puberty in math class. Instead, you were slavishly finding the area of a rhombus and calculating the angle Jane flies her kite with well-documented indifference. Whatever small currency these mechanical activities had then has long diminished to zero.

Seven minutes. The time it takes to make a soft-boiled egg. That's all that was required to save you thousands of dollars and have math work *for you* in this life. Mathematical expectation, as you will see, is a pint-sized concept with large implications. Understanding probability and its colorful history will save you money, but more importantly, save your waning interest in mathematics.

THE DEVIL'S MATH

Probability, which is at the heart of ME, has had a history of mystery, intrigue, and heated debate. And, even a simple concept like ME, perhaps has its reclusive roots linked to hundreds of years of false ideas and cultural battles that probability has endured. While there is ample evidence that dice have been around for thousands of years with links to recreational gambling, there is a no record of trying to come up with a mathematical model to explain probability during that time.

While the Greeks were comfortable with the notion of chance, it went against their nature to suppose that random events could be quantified in any useful fashion. They believed that any attempt to reconcile mathematically what did happen with what *should have* happened was, in their phraseology, an improper juxtaposition of the "earthly plane" with the "heavenly plane." This probably explains why there may have been no efforts, ironically, to quantify chance during this fertile period of mathematics.

Unfortunately, the next 1,500 years would provide a very harsh climate for probability to gain any serious footing, for as Christianity was broadening its influence, the idea of chance was considered heresy. It's easy to see that anyone who was brazen enough to challenge the Church's belief in fate with numerical analysis would have been burned upside down at the stake. It makes sense, then, that the first person who is given credit to reviving probability was a little bit of an eccentric nutcase.

Gerolamo Cardano was his name. He was born in 1501 and was a celebrated mathematician, physician, astrologer, and gambler. He was a true Renaissance man. He was the first person to describe typhoid fever and one of the first to believe that the deaf could communicate without learning to speak. Cardano also invented the combination lock, contributed to hydrodynamics, and wrote two encyclopedias on natural science. But like all good "crazy people," Cardano liked to color outside the lines. His writings were not always scholarly. While his gambling addictions did yield the first mathematical concepts of probability, he also had a whole section devoted to cheating. He even computed and wrote the horoscope of Christ in 1570, with jail being the reward for his lunatic endeavors.

But, for the man who is credited for the Lazarus-like resurrection of probability, there was one last thing to do to seal his fate as playing with a very short-handed deck—he predicted the *exact date of his death*. On September 21, 1576, Cardano died. This was supposedly the date he predicted, but he was also a known liar. Some even think he committed suicide to ensure his prognostication power left a mark.

Unfortunately, much of what Cardano might have contributed to probability was clouded by his strange personality. In fact, some of his more important contributions would not surface until 1654, years past the official birth of probability.

ROLL THE BONES

Chevalier de Mere, a professional gambler and amateur mathematician, conveyed his many questions about dice probability and outcomes to the great mathematician Blaise Pascal. Pascal, in turn, also sought counsel for these new mathematical questions. He turned to his good friend, Pierre de Fermat, another mathematical heavyweight. Together they began a systematic study of games of chance. The theory of probability was founded.

One of de Mere's questions was this: *What is the probability of throwing two dice and not getting a 1 or 6?* Pascal and Fermat alone were responsible for many rich and complex mathematical ideas, and yet they were tackling a relatively simple problem that should have been solved 1,000 years earlier. Concepts that paid homage to the beauty and complexity of a Creator of some kind had no problems thriving (geometry, infinity, etc.). Probability, on the other hand, had its evolution partially stunted for at least 2,000 years by being forced to share a bed with the devil.

But let's try to answer de Mere's question *without* knowing anything about probability. First, how many different combinations are there when two dice are thrown? We could start listing them like (1, 1), (1, 2), (2, 1), (2, 2), (2, 3), . . . We would soon discover there are 36 possibilities. A faster way would be to use something called the *Counting Principle* and simply multiply the total outcomes on each die—6 × 6 = 36.

So, of the 36 possibilities, how many don't have a 1 or a 6? Again, we could examine all our 36 outcomes and count all those that didn't have these numbers. Fortunately, our own language gives us the intuitive insight into a faster solution. The word *and* can be replaced by *multiply* and the word *or* by *addition*.

In this case, the probability of not throwing a 1 or 6 on the first die is four-sixths. The same can be said for the second die. So, we cannot get these two numbers on the first die *and* we cannot get these two numbers on the second die.

$$\frac{4}{6} \text{ AND } \frac{4}{6} \qquad \frac{4}{6} \times \frac{4}{6} = \frac{16}{36} = 0.44 = 44\%$$

With this information, de Mere knew he had the edge if he offered this game to people. For every 100 people playing this game, about 44 people would win and 56 people lose. If he charged them something like $1, he would collect $100 and pay out $44 \times \$2 = \$88$. A tidy profit of $12 would be made in this scenario. The first mathematically literate carnie was born! They would be better known as actuaries two centuries later.

THE CON JOB

While the birth of probability began with back-alley gambling, its influence would eventually become rich and broad. Over the next 300 years, probability would make advances into the areas of genetics, risk assessment, weather forecasting, game theory, and many more. However, the firming up of its mathematics has only occurred in the last 100 years.

Probability, compared to other mathematical ideas, is still an infant. This explains not only why its coverage in schools is erratic, but maybe why even supposedly informed sources fail to grasp the complete idea of probability. For example, brochures for disease foundation/hospital lotteries will trumpet ubiquitous lines like:

1 in 5 chances to win. Best odds!

This whole sentence is a mangled mess of misunderstanding and deception (the deception will be examined with more detail later in the chapter). To begin with, these numbers do not represent "odds." Odds are always related by two numbers: probability of an event occurring and the probability of it *not* occurring.

In the above example, 1 in 5 means you have one chance of winning and four chances of not winning. So, what should have been written was the *odds are 4 to 1 against you winning*. Charity lotteries disregard mathematical syntax for their own misleading purposes. Let's be honest here. Raising money for worthwhile causes is obviously a wonderful pursuit. However, things get murky when the advertising is mathematically false, only intended to mislead the customer.

The misuse of any language is shameful. Mathematics, sadly, is the uncontested leader in this department. Its unscrupulous tweaking is responsible for erasing all lines separating profits and ethics. Can you tell me another language that has billions of dollars tethered to its manipulation?

For even if these lotteries were consulted properly, part of me believes they would opt not to go with the correct presentation of odds. Why? Even though 4 to 1 ostensibly looks more appealing (4 is less than 5), the word "against" *must* be used here to correctly describe this chance situation. Lotteries, regardless of their good intentions, are all about putting on a dazzling smoke and mirrors show. All the advertising must be positive and ridiculously hopeful.

Against? Any word that might tickle the doubt regarding the overwhelming realities of such lotteries cannot be included. Are hospitals and charities allowed to raise money for the great causes they represent? Yes. But, as soon as they stop playing above board, their goals lose a lot of their philanthropic sheen. All this is moot, however, because the real play here is the deception of 1 in 5. While the inappropriate use of "odds" could be forgiven on a "toe-mato/tah-mato" scale, there is no room for cheek turning here. Just get ready to roll up your sleeves, folks!

Even the hit television show *NUMB3RS* failed to explore winning the lottery in terms of mathematical expectation. While the final analysis was couched in a clever fashion—if you buy 20 lottery tickets every week, it would take you 40,000 years to win the lottery—it still neglected the same principle at the center of every financial risk. Is it *worth* it?

THE STING OF MATHEMATICS

Back in early 2007, a representative of Primerica came to my house to discuss financial planning. Sandwiched between a glossy history of Primerica was the invitation to join their legal pyramid scheme—the MO of the sales reps is to sell life insurance. I'd been given newspaper articles about how mortgage insurance was a scam, so it didn't surprise me when the Primerica rep suggested adding my son to the policy for $15,000. It's one thing to have insurance for adults, it's quite another for children.

Was I supposed to treat the unexpected tragedy of my son as some kind of windfall worth the price of a used car? They could have added zeros until carpal tunnel syndrome was setting in, but my signature wasn't going to land on this unethical proposal.

Then, to make matters worse, despite the rep throwing out numbers and financial projections with apparent ease, he couldn't understand my simple explanation of mathematical expectation. It's like any logical rebuttal to buying insurance had not been programmed into his tight-as-a-drum pitch. The fact that this logic came served in cold, hard math was too sobering.

Soon enough the rep finished his well-rehearsed presentation with the same ending—"join us." No thanks.

While you'd be wise not to join a scam artist like the rep described above in his request, you'll be joining me and *ME* as you and your ilk are thrown to the mathematical lions in this chapter. Yes. If this chapter was going to have a soundtrack, it would be from the Clash or the Ramones.

THE CLASH OF INTUITION AND REALITY

So why did the Primerica guy fail to understand the concept of mathematical expectation? Well, it was probably more like he didn't *want* to understand it. (Plus, comprehending Primerica's deception would probably take a little wind out of making all those house calls.)

That's fine. For people working for companies like Primerica, learning about the truth would be disarming. For *us*, however, it will be the exact opposite. Mathematical expectation will clearly answer the question of any risk undertaking with the subtlety of a cross bolt to the forehead. While you may not need the help of its simple formula to come up with your own answers regarding money and risk—namely, "no, it's not worth it"—you will not be able to punctuate your calculation with the same force as ME.

In other words, you may be smart enough to know that casinos, insurance, and lotteries are a rip-off, but you just don't have the tool to figure out by how much. Let's start with a very simple question on probability. And don't feel bad if you don't know the answer. Probability can be quite tricky. Many math teachers and math majors give incorrect answers! Here is the question:

A mother tells her friend she has two children.
She says she has at least one girl.
What is the probability she has two girls?
(insert Final Jeopardy music . . .)

If you said something like 50/50, half, or 1 in 2, you would be wrong.

Intuition and the question itself points you in the wrong direction—boy/girl, 1 girl/2 girls, etc. There are other variations of this question that egg you on toward the false answer of 50 percent. The correct answer?

In 1998, I started teaching at Riverdale High School. The first day of school I found myself mildly disoriented near the staff mailbox—looking for my slot among the din of arriving teachers doing the enthusiastic September greetings.

During a break in the commotion, I met a fellow newbie to the school. Like a European sports car, my conversation—more like rant—went from benign pleasantries to a scathing condemnation of math education. When I stopped (because I needed air), this middle-aged, British gentleman simply said, "We'll talk . . ."

His name was Peter Harrison. I did not know at the time, but I was talking to one of the greatest math teachers that I would ever come across. He even visited my classroom in Switzerland! Needless to say, we have kept talking . . .

One of the brilliant things Peter used to do in his classrooms was to assign these really difficult math problems. But, students could ask anyone for help, including fellow students, other teachers—even university professors. They just couldn't ask him.

Peter's goal was not to have students find the correct solution; Peter's goal was to help students figure out *where* to find the correct solution. He wanted the mathematics to leave the classroom/school and percolate in the outside world. He wanted to fan the flames of mathematical initiative and curiosity. He literally wanted his students to take math for a walk outside the limiting walls of a classroom and search for answers anywhere and everywhere—sort of like a mathematics version of Pokémon GO!

Search out this innocent puzzle and it's *not-so-innocent* answer. You will be glad you did! (*Hint: Google "James Tanton."*)

Do not for one second underestimate the profiteering potential that is symbolized in this "cute puzzle." When a good chunk of the population is offering up 50 percent as the answer, a sizeable gulf is now created between what people perceive as the probability and what the actual probability is—this is one of the main ways people get exploited by lotteries and insurance.

As you will see, these kinds of percentages translate into billions of dollars when fairness is believed but never comes close to existing. The total weight of our inability to grasp even the most fundamental mathematical laws is leaving the door open for numerical mischief and manipulation by corporations.

Our failure to understand probability becomes a bottomless money trough for many industries. This financial nirvana only exists because our general mathematical illiteracy is so entrenched and prevalent in society. After a while, taking full advantage of the consumer's numerical shortcomings will become nothing short of stealing—especially when all that is being sold is a service manipulating our desires or fears.

GREAT EXPECTATIONS

Perhaps the best way to explain ME is to discuss *value*. Any time you play the lottery, purchase insurance, or buy a warranty, you are putting money in (your loss) in the hopes of getting money/risk protection out (your gain).

Value Lost + Value Gain = Net Value

We can surely see the money we spend and we know what we will get if we win (a million dollars, free repairs, a new television, etc.), but is it enough information to determine if this risk is fair? We need to arm ourselves with the knowledge of probability.

Let's take a simple task like flipping a coin and turning it into a betting game. In order for ME to do its job, we need to provide three pieces of information. If we do, then all it asks from us is that we can multiply fractions.

1. The Cost to Play
2. The Amount to Be Won
3. The Probability of Winning

That is why the mathematically based show *NUMB3RS* failed to completely analyze playing the lottery—it didn't factor in the financial stakes of the first two criteria. If it did, it would have shown that it is quite possible to play the lottery and produce the holy grail of probability—a positive expectation! Yes, its verdict with regards to playing the lottery was correct in terms of sheer futility. However, it conveniently ignored a crucial piece of evidence that would have, at the very least, tempered its smart and somewhat smug conclusion. But before we discover what everyone overlooks, we need to take some baby steps first. So, let's get back to the coin toss.

1. The Cost to Play $1
2. The Amount to Be Won $1
3. The Probability of Winning $\frac{1}{2}$

So, we can now expand our Net Value equation.

Value Lost + Value Gain = Net Value
(Probability of Loss × Loss) + (Probability of Gain × Gain)
= Expected Value

Expected Value is your mathematical expectation. In theory, you should only play games in which the ME is positive. However, even this is not a sufficient condition to gamble. Mathematical expectation is what you should expect in the *long run*. (Often, this "long run" can well exceed the lifetime expectancy of humans.) While the show *NUMB3RS* was slightly negligent in its research into the mathematics of a lottery, it did give a stark reality of the time line for anyone of us to profit from playing the lottery.

Yes, the ME of a typical draw game is decent, and as mentioned earlier, positive on occasions. But, none of us will even live to see half of one percent of the expectation time line of 40,000 years. So, not only must the ME be positive, but the period of time that it defines has to be practical.

The only game that this can occur on a somewhat regular basis is blackjack. The problem is that you should also have the bankroll, patience, concentration, knowledge, and wits to capitalize on it. The MIT Blackjack Team that ran for almost 15 years didn't have this problem. They used their knowledge of mathematics against the casinos—and won. Their fascinating story was well documented in the best seller *Bringing Down the House*.

Nevertheless, aside from the perfect, yet transient, conditions of blackjack and rare lottery situations, every ME you will encounter in this life is negative—many times *very* negative. But, let's see how our coin toss turned out.

$$(P_l \times L) + (P_g \times G) = ME$$

$$-(\frac{1}{2} \times \$1) + (\frac{1}{2} \times \$1) = ME$$

$$-50 \text{ cents} + 50 \text{ cents} = 0$$

Mathematical expectation is telling us that this game will produce zero profit over the long run. In a simple game like this, our common sense is in perfect alignment with mathematics. While you can bet on a coin toss for the Super Bowl, you will be obliged to pay some kind of "juice"—the commission to the bookie who takes these bets.

But this juice is reasonable, visible, understood, and accepted. So, even though the expectation is rendered negative in theory by this commission, professional gamblers feel they can use sports knowledge and trends to overcome the juice they are laying out (except on a coin toss).

Lottery "juice," on the other hand, is unreasonable, invisible, misunderstood, and yet *still accepted. Math 101? Everyday Math for Dummies?* The lecture/chapter on ME in these books seems to be mysteriously absent.

PENNIES SAVED IS A HOTEL EARNED

Gambling is a source of pleasure and excitement for many people. And casinos around the world want you to have fun, but it's going to cost you—but not as much as you might think. Most casino games have a negative expectation of 2 to 5 cents per dollar wagered. That's how much you can expect to lose for every dollar wagered over time. That might not seem like a lot, but Mother always said "count your pennies."

Las Vegas took that advice and used mathematical laws of expectation and large numbers to build itself into the opulent state that it is today. Casinos operate 24/7 for a reason—to ensure that mathematics is always on their side. Yes, there are winners in Vegas, but in the short term only. Outside of the MIT gang, which perfected card-counting and betting strategies, very few people can "break" Vegas over a long period of time. Why?

It is mathematically impossible.

Here's some proof: winners didn't build the Bellagio; losers did. While the games that casinos offer are unfair, the average person is willing to chalk up this mathematical disadvantage to the price to be entertained. Las Vegas is very sensitive to this as they are quick to ditch games that, while having a bigger profit margin (higher negative expectation), don't attract the critical mass of players needed to make the desired profit.

A game that is played by thousands every minute, but makes only a few cents on the dollar, will outperform a game with higher return but low player turnout. There are times that certain promotions for games will yield positive expectations, and smart players will capitalize on them before the casinos figure out the discrepancy. Of all the industries that use ME, casinos are the fairest—albeit their altruism is a reflection, paradoxically in a sense, of their selfishness to make money.

But casinos are smarter than they are selfish. Besides having the *Law of Large Numbers*—the mathematical idea that after thousands of trials, the experimental probability will match the theoretical probability—in their back pocket, casinos are very careful to examine even the subtlest aspects of their games. Craps, for example, is a very popular game, constantly surfing any Bond mythology that it has been given over the years.

The ME of craps is on par with most other casino games. Despite its calculation involving only the multiplication and addition of fractions, its computation remains beyond the reach of even the brightest high school math students. Complicated math that is memorized is an easier task than basic math that requires . . . thinking.

What makes craps such an interesting game from an ME perspective is the actual dice that are used. The dice? These are not the dice you find in any board game like Monopoly or Trivial Pursuit. Casino dice are the *fairest* dice on the planet. Ironically, we all use "crooked" dice when we play recreational games—casinos don't!

The dice used in craps have two key features not found in regular dice: sharp corners and completely smooth surfaces (figure 7.1). The dimples normally seen on household die are nonexistent in craps, which have the dots painted on.

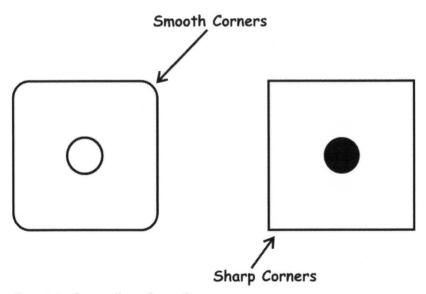

Figure 7.1. Crappy die vs. Craps die.

So what? Isn't that what you're thinking? But, these little pits on the surfaces (technical term is *pips*) represent mass taken out of the die. Therefore, the "six" has the most dice taken out. As such, it is the lightest side. The "one," which is on the opposite side, is the heaviest as it has only one indentation.

It has been proven statistically that over several thousand rolls there will be a slight bias toward a die of this construction landing on its lightest side—the six. In any board game that lasts a few hours, there might be several hundred rolls of the dice. Not only is this not enough data to warrant any concern about how the game turned out, but most board games are played with zero stakes among friends.

Casinos, however, will have their dice rolled thousands of times with money always on the line. Any quirk, however small, must be eliminated, as it will always creep into and affect the outcome of their games. Here casinos are employing detailed analysis of probability and statistics to ensure optimum conditions for the house. Smart? You bet. But, there are times when casinos will play "dumb" and purposefully use a common fallacy about probability—that past random events affect the future.

The only game in which history has bearing on the future outcome is blackjack—hence, the whole business of card counting. Where casinos pretend to be slaves to the historical ignorance of chance is at the roulette wheel. If you have ever been to the casino you might notice that there is a brightly lit board beside a roulette wheel keeping track of all the numbers the roulette ball has landed on. This serves no other purpose than for patrons to falsely analyze the board for trends and bet with or against certain numbers.

THE EXTENDED WARRANTY LESSON

Casinos have a lethal mix for unstoppable profits—the lure of gambling, small negative expectation for its bettors, large volume of players, and a strong mathematical rooting section. No other industry operates under such ideal financial conditions to exploit mathematical expectation in a relatively—dare I say it—*fair way.*

Playing second fiddle to the intoxicating rush of gambling is our general fear of things going wrong for us. This is where insurance companies come in and, *unlike a good neighbor*, they are never there for you. Insurance is basically a financial tool used by people to protect themselves from a potentially bigger loss. The individual pays a small amount over time to insulate themselves from harm and damage to their possessions or to themselves.

Insurance agencies have very skilled mathematicians (actuaries) who determine things like frequency and amount of the payouts and likelihood of fraudulent claims. Once this is determined, a *hefty* profit margin is calculated, and this is translated into the premiums consumers pay. Bottom line: it is *never* worth buying insurance. Your mathematical expectation will always be soaked in blood red. Your obligations toward insurance should only be legal or, in rare circumstances, ethical.

But, you might say something like "what if something happens . . ."? Oh, yes. *What if* . . . The nervous, society-induced mantra to frighten the public. Selling fear and unfavorable mathematics for the consumer are like peaches and cream for the insurance industry.

"What if" will always be trounced by the premium you are paying to play these insurance games. This isn't blackjack or craps where mathematical expectation exists near the oasis of zero expectation. This is mathematical hell. It's not your pennies that are in danger with insurance—health, dental, travel, credit card balance, auto, life, etc. No. Losing mere cents will not generate the profits that these companies greedily desire. They are banking on the fact that your fear of calamity coupled with mathematical ignorance will allow for a deep well to be drilled into your bank account.

Think about it. We are conditioned to constantly hand over our money to protect us from the least likely of events. Peace of mind? Sure. At what cost, though? Entertainment yields fairness; yet our personal well-being yields cheating. This is indeed a *mad, mad, mad, mad world*. And, as we will discover at the end of this chapter, the people we trust the most—the government—are the biggest cheaters in our financial lives.

For example, let's say you want to buy a Hewlett-Packard printer/scanner/fax machine at Best Buy.

The funny thing is that the Consumer Association of Canada has been telling consumers for years that buying an extended warranty is *unnecessary*. That isn't the strongest language to use if what you are advising against is so clearly in the retailer's favor. But, unsurprisingly, CAC couldn't back up their advice with anything convincing other than grandfatherly type wisdom. Simply put, where was the mathematical beef?

Without it, all CAC could muster was a well-intentioned opinion. Had anyone in the organization learned about ME, the *opinion* would have been transformed into *fact*.

The printer in question is $300. As you complete your purchase, the sales clerk reaches for the ubiquitous glossy brochure—the extended warranty guarantee. If a company is spending money on slick foldouts of promise and warranties—usually prefaced by valuable elements like gold, silver, or platinum—then we should be on *DEFCON 1* in terms of the swindle that is being manufactured. Platinum warranty = platinum profits.

Next, you might ask the sales clerk, "What can I win if I purchase this warranty?"

After a few seconds of understandable silence, the clerk might mutter, "A new printer?"

See, once you know the price of the printer ($300), there's only one more number to fill in the ME formula—the probability of the printer breaking down over the next three years.

Hewlett-Packard is a large multinational corporation with profits in the billions. Coupling that reality with the fact that standard manufacturing defect of a product usually sits at 1 to 2 percent, setting the probability breakdown at 10 percent would yield a lot of complaints. The shareholders at HP would not be happy campers! Considering this, you set the probability at 5 percent (still high).

$$ME = 1/20 \times \$300 = \$15$$

In the end, you'd "win" 15 bucks.

With this knowledge, you might then ask the sales clerk, "What's the cost of this warranty?"

At this point, the clerk might blush as he answers, "$60.00."

$$\$15 - \$60 = -\$45$$

Wow, that turns out to be a *minus 75 percent expectation*. Ten times worse than the shadiest casino game.

Another way to look at this ruse is to imagine even only 20 people signing up for this warranty. Best Buy then collects 20 × $60 = $1,200. Out of the 20 printers it has sold, only 1 out of 20 will likely suffer malfunction over the next three years. Best Buy must spend $300 to replace this defective machine. In case you missed it, they just pocketed a cool $900 for doing nothing but offering a service with some very unsavory mathematics.

The Simpsons—a show now well known for its think tank of writers that hold degrees in mathematics (thanks to Simon Singh's revealing book, *The Mathematical Secrets of* The Simpsons)—nailed this whole extended warranty nonsense over a decade ago. Constantly ahead of its time (the show predicted the Trump presidency in 2000), it's *not* remarkable to think that *The Simpsons'* multi-layering commentary/comedic gold/satire was hatched in the equally complex brains of world-class mathematicians.

In season 12 of *The Simpsons*, there is a scene in which Homer is exhausted from being smart and wants to be dumb again. So, Dr. Nick Riviera starts hammering a crayon back up his nose to his brain. Homer's first response to indicate that this quack surgery was a success? "Extended Warranty. How Can I Lose?"

CIGARETTES, TRANS FAT, AND GOVERNMENT LOTTERIES

In early 2007, Canada's largest government-run lottery, the Ontario Lottery Corporation (OLC), was broadsided with a much-publicized scandal that was part of an investigative report by the highly acclaimed news show *The Fifth Estate*. At the center of the controversy was that lottery retailers and families had "won" an astonishing 200 times over a seven-year period—a number that was astronomically high for sheer chance, according to a University of Toronto statistician. The prizes varied from $50,000 to over a million.

The OLC, which rakes in several billion dollars a year in revenue, took many steps soon after to allay fears of questionable integrity in the over 30 games of chance it offers. It fired several six-figure-earning drones, and introduced safety features to ensure that winners would not be cheated out of their winnings. To what degree retailers were collecting prizes pales in comparison to the scandal that should have been reported: in my opinion, the OLC uses and abuses the mathematical expectation of winning in all its games in a monopolistic and predatory environment. It seems that their primary intention is to maximize profits with an unethical, well-orchestrated scheme that is undetectable to the public.

Yes. This is a substantial charge. However, there is damning evidence everywhere to support these allegations—including the Ontario Lottery and Gaming (OLG) website. A few weeks after the fraud and insider winning allegations became public knowledge, the minister of finance was on television at a convenience store doing the grossly obvious: purchasing a lottery ticket. He was asked on camera if people should play the lottery. With a tilt of the head upward, the minister let out a mugging guffaw followed by a very reassuring "of course they should."

Interesting. Would the government feel as comfortable with the minister of health going on television and being asked if people should smoke cigarettes or eat doughnuts for breakfast and responding with the same ridiculous remark? Of course not.

They know that the public is fully educated to the dangers of nicotine and trans fat. The government only thinks the public is stupid when it comes to *math*, not science. And, in at least the case of physical health, the government sides with the public. But, more important, most have no more knowledge about dangers of all the carcinogenic chemicals in a cigarette or the sugar and fat content in fried dough than us.

Similarly, as was with manufacturers of tobacco and now more recently with food companies, the dangers of nicotine and trans fats have been acknowledged by their producers with either warnings and/or removal of the harmful elements. Philip Morris and Kraft are not terribly concerned about our health, but more about the possibility of lawsuits if they knowingly "poisoned" consumers with their products. We may continue to smoke and consume fatty foods, but we always are aware of the outcomes of such indulgences.

We *understand* the negative expectations of such lifestyle choices. We, however, rarely understand the negative expectations when the lifestyle choice involves gambling. Thank you, math education.

All government lotteries not only efficiently exploit our inability to see the *mathematical trans fat*, but through cavalier marketing techniques, they cajole, dupe, coax, and entice a large portion of the public to play their rigged games. Even if 75 percent of the billions of dollars generated through this illicit operation went to build hospitals and charitable causes—which it doesn't—the government has long breached its trust with the public.

Of the millions of people who get bilked of their hard-earned money every year, how many of them directly benefit from the good deeds of lottery profits? The citizens of the province of Ontario, like most provinces and states, already pay a large tax that should cover many of the social services needed by a society.

When government lotteries mature into a corporation making brontosaurus-like profits, scandals like the one the OLC was afflicted with should not be shocking. They should be inevitable. It's time to venture inside and look at the manipulative machinery that is the government lottery.

BUY ONE TICKET ONLY

Almost all casino games operate with about a 5 percent house edge. Again, that means for every dollar you wager, you will lose about a nickel in the long run. Factoring in the fun factor of gambling, being in a casino, complimentary drinks, and such, these games are very fair.

Government-run lotteries, which somehow escape antitrust lawsuits with their refusal of any competition, have negative expectations from 30 to 50 percent in all their games! And, every single piece of advertising, promotion, and marketing is governed by increasing this negative expectation with one very simple trick: encourage "group" play.

If you are going to play the lottery, only buy *one* ticket! If you purchase any more than that you are simply increasing your negative expectation and playing right into the slippery hands of the government. In a 6/49 game, you must pick 6 numbers out of 49 to win the jackpot. There are about 14 million combinations of these 6 numbers. If you buy one ticket, you have . . . tada! . . . 1 chance in *14 million*.

Let's say the jackpot is at $14 million and the cost of the ticket is $1. The mathematical expectation of playing under these conditions is roughly zero. Yes, there are secondary prizes, but to underscore the number where it becomes tactical to play this lottery, the jackpot should be about $14 million.

Heck, for the fantasizing around the work watercooler of what you would do with your millions, buying one ticket as a lark provides mental entertainment for a day or two. If you don't buy a ticket, you have zero chance of winning. And, while 1 out of 14 million is close to zero, you at least have the privilege of daydreaming about being on a Caribbean beach for the rest of your life.

Buying more than one ticket is . . . well . . . not a wise choice. Remember, the government spends a lot of money on lottery advertising ensuring that we do things that are in the best interest of them, not us. So, let's pretend that your little office group buys 20 tickets at a dollar a pop as described on the *NUMB3RS* show.

$$- (20) + (20/14000000 \times 14000000) = 0$$

Neglecting the smaller prizes, your expectation is the same as buying one ticket! Why would you pay $20 to chase a rabbit down a hole, when you can do the same for a cheap buck? You have increased your investment by 1,900 percent to increase your chances of winning the jackpot from 0.0000007 percent to a whopping 0.0000014 percent!

The government is right. You do increase your chances of winning—in decimal amounts that are statistically insignificant. The expected value of playing the lottery is immaterial—you will be long dead before you can break even.

So, while technically group play doesn't change the result of the expectation, it realistically snatches every dollar you contribute. Your expectation is only zero if you can somehow get cryogenics to work. Your expectation, otherwise, is equal to whatever you contribute with a big fat negative sign in front of it.

Granted, you have more chances of winning the smaller and insignificant prizes like $10 (the rubber duckies of the lotto world), but this isn't going to put a meaningful dent into your whopping negative expectation by any means. You will always be better off with one ticket.

For why else would the government spend thousands on advertising trying to improve *your* financial expectation?

In fact, a few years back there was a blitz of television ads announcing the new Lotto 6/49. The commercials were basically this loud conga line navigating through suburban streets trumpeting the arrival of a bigger and better lottery with more prizes. At the end of the commercial, it was mentioned that it costs $2 to play. It used to be $1—such bombast that only resulted in, yup, a higher negative expectation for everyone to play these already fruitless lotteries.

It's all about mathematical expectation. Distract, hide, and amuse are just ways to make the government's apple with the worm a little shinier. The play-as-a-group scenario is really about pushing your expectation more into the red. Encouraging something so detrimental to your financial health is disgusting.

The other reason the government wants you to start a group of lotto players is that there is a psychological commitment to the group. Once you start to ante up your coffee change every week, you might feel obliged to do so, well, kind of forever. (The fear of your coworkers showing up to work in BMWs after a jackpot could scare all the mathematical common sense right out of you.)

It's worth mentioning that there is also no class barrier for mathematical ignorance. Even well-healed people purchase an ungodly number of tickets. For proof, let's revisit *The Simpsons*. Fifteen years ago, there was a *Simpsons* episode where Homer purchased 50 lottery tickets for the $130 million jackpot. He said, "With so many tickets, I can't lose!" As soon as one number is drawn, almost all of Homer's tickets are useless and he starts ripping them up. His daughter Lisa then correctly informs him that he can win secondary prizes. The next number is drawn, and Homer's famous utterance of *Doh!*—a linguistic staple in Oxford's online dictionary for over five years—signals his foolishness and frustration with his wasted investment.

Unlike Homer, we never really learned our lesson. And this is due to our general disobedience of mathematical truths and sinister tactics by lottery strategists to lure us into their bee-infested honey pot. Primerica house calls, extended warranty brochures, and now lottery advertising are stern warnings to us that something rotten is afoot. Tobacco advertising is all but dead in North America, but lottery advertising by trusted government officials can run rampant?

Stripped of all its gloss, hopeful television and print ads, state lotteries are very much like those unsavory carnies who hustle us into believing that our ring will fit around a peg. This is where math education must step up and stop handing out butter knives of application and safety scissors of knowledge and start teaching mathematics that hack into the hegemony of society. Failing that, benign and diversionary mathematics will remain the status quo.

We need to arm our future generations with shields and swords to do battle with those who feast off mathematical illiteracy. Critical math equals critical thinking. Decision-making mathematics that involves optimal strategy of game theory is a good a place to start—and at a young age.

What do you think is involved in a game like hide-and-seek? Calculation of distance, speed, and quality of cover are the parameters covered ever so lightheartedly by laughing children.

For now, a collective criticism of what and how we are taught needs to be our focus. Why is it all right for the government to promote gambling recklessly, but within the institution of education—a government stronghold—the discussion of it in an academic manner is verboten. Do they still read *Fahrenheit 451* in English classes? Mathematical expectation is, and always will be, far more critical to the lives of people than, let's say, the quadratic formula. The quadratic formula gets several hours of attention. Even with ground-floor derivation, it's not particularly useful—about as useful as an eleven-sixteenths-inch wrench with three-quarter-inch bolts.

Mathematical expectation? Never even gets a fraction of the attention in most math curriculums around the world. Again, you do the math. *Money math*, that is. If people were exposed to mathematics in high school that could uncover wrongdoing, elicit rich discussions on risk and zero-sum games, and stir their souls with vibrant history, then perhaps a generation of learners could be created that love mathematics.

Instead, we continue to produce generation after generation of students who loathe math. But far worse, is that we always pretend to care and then spend millions on remedies that are placebos in disguise—new math strategies with old topics.

The power of razor-sharp mathematics is indisputable. Combine that with the argumentative powers of logic and proof, and you have the template for society developing a new mind-set for mathematics that involves critiquing the institutions that intersect our lives. But, the true power of mathematics is its lifetime gift of happiness, the measure of which can only be ascertained if it *somehow* becomes the only happiness available outside of family and friends.

CHAPTER 8

ABC'd

Resilience

> When we rob people of their pain—when we don't allow them the
> possibility of failure—we also rob them of their happiness.
>
> —*Eric Greitens*

In the most famous scene of the 1960 film *Spartacus*, the defeated iconic character, played by the chiseled Kirk Douglas, yields to the defeat of his slave army. The captured army has been given freedom on the condition that the identity of this now mythical man be revealed. The gas tank of resolve is empty for Douglas's heroic protagonist. It is not, however, for his army, as they all start standing up one by one and trumpeting that they are indeed Spartacus. There is nothing manufactured here. It's all an organic reaction to the summation of experience. Drawing upon defiance and solidarity after a defeat is the movie's homage to resilience.

Thirty-four years later, at the age of 80, Kirk Douglas would suffer a debilitating stroke that should have steered his remaining years into a quiet anonymity of hospice life. It didn't. This time, in real life, Kirk Douglas did not yield to defeat—especially since this battle was solely personal and private. In *Spartacus*, he wielded a sword. In his post-stroke life, he chose to wield a pen. The mightier pen was the triumphant instrument here, as he referred to his medical setback as a gift.

The life lessons that Douglas refers to throughout the book *My Stroke of Luck* all emanate from the familiar narrative of loss, defeat, suffering, or impoverishment embedding a tensile nature in humans. The resilience that flowered in one of Hollywood's most beloved actors would be charmingly recounted in the book. Resilience, through its own strange emotional alchemy, takes us from darkness and despair into an everlasting light that would not have been seen without the setback.

Much like curiosity, resilience has had its own integral part in our happiness, which has been fleshed out in whole books. Resilience, as Greitens cites in his book *Resilience: Hard-Won Wisdom for Living a Better Life* is eternal wisdom that goes unheeded today. It is a virtue that enables one to lead a fuller and happier life—especially when we must go through some dark and difficult times.

THE REQUIREMENT OF RESILIENCE IN MATHEMATICS

Mathematics has been filled with men and women who demonstrated much resilience in trying to unravel the mysteries of the universe. To dedicate almost their entire lives to pondering a single question—with no guarantee of success and to usually suffer in isolated margins—is resilience of the mind, body, and soul. Andrew Wiles, who cracked the 350-year-old Fermat problem—a problem essentially that basically said "nothing past Pythagoras"—was lauded by the global mathematical community for his remarkable breakthrough. What many did not know is the amount of despair he went through with the problem that had captivated him since childhood, which bordered on a nervous breakdown.

The stories of mathematical resilience are worth telling for the sole reason of making mathematics a human endeavor that crosses all lines of race, culture, gender, and class. And, while a significant price is often paid to be drawn into the often tangled web of math, much empathy for its devotees can be found, empathy that shades mathematics with a universal connectedness.

Resilience is, unfortunately, not really a skill that is acquired, honed, or practiced. You cannot go to a workshop on resilience. It's not an external exercise. It's an internal gift. Kirk Douglas devoted a whole book for framing a potentially debilitating stroke as a gift. The real name of his gift was resilience. The only way to receive this gift is to suffer a personal setback through failure. It doesn't mean it's guaranteed, it is just a prerequisite condition.

Around 2,500 years ago, Pythagoras put his stamp on the unique relationship of sides of a 90-degree triangle. Although there is strong evidence now that countries like India and China had independently discovered this iconic relationship of $a^2 + b^2 = c^2$. For more than three and half centuries after Fermat posed his now "enigma" in 1637—that there would be no solutions outside the "square world"—did various generations of mathematicians take swings at this nasty *slider*. Everyone struck out. While there is obviously no documentation of this, most of the attempts probably occurred in a recreational time frame of a few days to a few months.

What was the longest time that you spent on one math problem in school? Would it be safe to say it was less than a few days? Most students today lack any stick-to-itiveness with mathematics. A deadly merging of antiquated questions, contrived narratives, and disinterested resolutions has something to do with this. Resilience doesn't develop in these conditions with yawning 10-minute attempts. Mathematical apathy, however, sure does.

As mentioned in chapter 3, Andrew Wiles spent seven lonely years in what some might call a self-imprisonment trying to prove the oldest, unsolved problem in mathematics. The fact that he spiraled into bouts of depression indicates that his resilience was beyond heroic. Even marathon runners succumb to fatigue. Fatigue? Wiles was eating that for breakfast. He marched on even when his mental stability was in danger. He could have called it quits and he still might have been more than a footnote in mathematical lore.

Hmmmph. The first three innocent letters of the alphabet. Each having an easily understood superscript of a two. The overall relationship now a good part of our cultural vernacular, replete with many visual reinforcements. Introduce an imaginative thought about the boundaries of this relationship in the Renaissance era and you create magic, mayhem, and madness. Above all, you create the longevity of resilience, with a formal coronation in 1993.

A NEW HEADACHE FOR MATH

One of the sad and enduring myths of mathematics that is passively accepted by most is that mathematics is cold, dead, and all discovered. Since most high school mathematics peak in ninth-century India—save for statistics and calculus—the myth mightily lives on. Most of us experienced very little math history. Couple that with absolutely no mention of current endeavors and future goals—as ridiculously abstract as they might be—sets up mathematics as the immaculate conception of knowledge.

Some of the world's most brilliant mathematicians go over the moon when new ideas, conjectures, and theories are presented, even if they have no understanding as to what is being communicated. If your ability in mathematics ever eclipses your love for mathematics then *both* are doomed.

A few years before Wiles was going to undertake his odyssey, another *"abc"* relationship was brewed up. In 1985, Oesterle and Masser conjectured something complex and abstract from the most innocent and simple idea: a + b = c.

First, *a*, *b*, and *c* are whole numbers. However, they do not share any common factors—that is, they are coprime. For example, $15 + 28 = 43$. The prime factors of 15 are 5×3. The factors of 28 are $2 \times 2 \times 7$. And 43 is a prime number. Every number, broken down into its building-block prime components, shares none of them with the other numbers. Now count the prime factors on the left side and the right side.

$$3 \times 5 + 2 \times 2 \times 7 = 43$$

The left side is rich in prime factors. A total of five of them. The right side has only one. And this is what you get most of the time—left-heavy number of primes. Pretty straightforward at this point, but please stay on the path! There are exceptions. How about $7 + 121 = 128$? First, let's make sure that everything is copasetic with our coprime restriction.

$$7 + 11 \times 11 = 2 \times 2 \times 2 \times 2 \times 2 \times 2 \times 2$$

Roger that! Now, let's confirm what our eyes already see—that the right side has more prime factors. The left has three and the right has a boasting seven! Again, this is the exception. Have you noticed that any time there has been a deeper plunge into the sea of math, it's always been about the topic of number theory? It's intrinsically fascinating and has enormous implications in continuing to unlock the mysteries of the mathematical unknown.

This takes us to the end of our tour in terms of the *abc* conjecture. If, in our first example, we multiply together all the unique primes—2 × 3 × 5 × 7 × 43—we get something called the radical of *abc*. In this case, the answer is 9,030. This is bigger than 43, which if you remember is *c*. In general, this is usually true, but there are exceptions. How many? Unlimited. Infinite. More formally written, the statement reads: rad(abc) > c. Our mini mathematical hike is over, but the journey of this problem is the stuff of great science fiction—or, I suppose in this case, *math fiction.*

Only half the conjecture was given. The other half involves the *abc* bracket being raised to an exponent larger than the inconsequential "one." Even if it is a smidgen over this fundamental number, the number of exceptions is no longer infinite. They are finite. You can count them all. The problem is not that no one has discovered a proof for this infant of a conjecture. The problem is that somebody *has*—and literally nobody else understands what the hell is going on.

Shinichi Mochizuki unveiled his 500-page proof in 2012. Most proofs undergo a one- to two-year verification process by other mathematicians. Four years later, not only has the progress been frustrating, it got punctuated with the following headline in www.nature.com: "Monumental Proof to Torment Mathematicians for Years to Come."

The crux of the problem here is that Mochizuki has introduced a field of mathematics that, guess what, only he understands—*Inter-Universal Teichmuller* theory (IUT). If this was the field of astronomy, it would sound like he figured out how to travel through wormholes in outer space to other universes. Astonishingly, that is what he has done in the field of mathematics! Forget the fact that it will take years for even the brightest math minds to learn this new branch of math; they will also have to be prepared to *unlearn* other branches of mathematics. It is why very few people have the guts to go on this black hole adventure—it is literally a journey of darkness with the slowest of illumination.

But, we wouldn't be here if not for the resilience of Mochizuki. (Specifically, about two decades' worth of resilience.) There are lots of unsolved problems in math. Some just carry greater cache based on when they got hatched and what kind of history has been drawn from them. However, there are valuable lessons to be unpacked here. Benjamin Braun, editor in chief at the American Mathematical Society

Blogs, is one such person who is using *impenetrability* to normalize failure—the engine of resilience. He wrote a blog post called "Famous Unsolved Problems as Homework":

> Because working on unsolved problems forces success to be redefined, it also provides an opportunity to discuss the definition of failure, and the pervasive normality of small mistakes in the day-to-day lives of mathematicians and scientists.

What is interesting about some of the unsolved problems that Braun assigns is that their understanding and churning out of results involves an only elementary school understanding of math. For example, the Collatz Conjecture, first proposed by Luther Collatz in 1937, is a charming little bifurcation of odd and even numbers. Pick any number, n. If n is odd, put it through the function $3n + 1$ If it is even, calculate $n/2$. Whatever number you get, put it through the same filter of operations based on if the number is odd or even. Let's put a couple of numbers to the test:

$$17: 52, 26, 13, 40, 20, 10, 5, 16, 8, 4, 2, 1$$
$$38: 19, 58, 29, 88, 44, 22, 11, 34, 17, 52, 26, 13, 40, 20, 10, 5, 16, 8, 4, 2, 1$$

See what happened? They both ended at 1. This is what the conjecture states. Every number will eventually cycle its way down to the unit number, 1.

As you can probably guess, some of the larger numbers will have sequences of several thousand steps. Regardless, they will all terminate to 1. What you might not have guessed is that since all numbers eventually go to 1—the root—something called a Collatz map of all the sequences and their common branch points will produce an image that looks very much like the roots of a plant or a tree. The beautiful fractal! Number theory is a catch basin for not only developing rigorous problem solving but for discovering mathematical surprises.

But, is resilience the same in every condition? Does bouncing back from a physical or emotional setback have anything to do with resilience found in the darkness of mathematical irresolution? This question would be answered over a two-year period. It literally started with a knock on my door . . .

I had just finished lunch and started walking toward my classroom for my grade 11 remedial class. They would not be expecting me.

I was supposed to be in an in-school workshop for the very class that was being supported for success. I had missed too many classes attending these benign attempts of student understanding of math. My students were getting weary of substitute teachers.

I decided not to attend the last installment of these workshops—hosted by my home school.

Barely 10 minutes into the class, there was a knock on my door. It was the principal. He asked me why I wasn't in the library with the other teachers in the "Student Success" workshop. I told him that I needed to be with my students. My lack of emotion in my answer hinted at what was about to come.

In the most admonishing way possible, he said "Sunil, please see me first thing tomorrow morning."

(Snap.) It took mere seconds to formulate my response.

I came to the office early the next day. Around 7:30 a.m. if I do remember correctly. The principal showed up just before 8 a.m. He seemed surprised to see me so punctual for what was obviously going to be a stern reprimand. A few minutes later, I would be sitting across from him. He started his grievances about my refusal to attend the workshop. I gave him about a minute to get his "noose" around my neck. I then said in the least audible "stop" I could say, projecting a tranquility with what I was about to say.

"I quit." I handed him my resignation letter that I had spent the night writing. It was seven pages long. I walked out of his office and down the hall to my first class.

I was no longer unhappy . . .

In his 2012 address to graduating MBA students, Deepak Malhotra told them that "quitting takes more strength than perseverance." Perhaps Malhotra underestimated that when *unhappiness* gets stirred with late-blooming *idealism*, a powerful cocktail is created.

It's clear that mental toughness can spring forth from mathematics, from hours upon hours of doing problems in the *jungle*. Do you know the jungle? Axl Rose wrote a song about it—"Welcome to the Jungle." If there was ever going to be a rock and roll song to describe the heart and soul of mathematical problem solving, Guns N' Roses penned it!

Satisfying and character-building problem solving doesn't come easy. In fact, the end game is often just how many hours of frustration you clocked in. The solution—*aka the escape*—is satisfying, but the "chase is always better than the catch."

MATHEMATICAL CUTS AND SCRAPES

Good math problems are ones you don't know how to do. And there are good math problems all the way from kindergarten to grade 12. Everyone should experience resistance in cobbling together their solutions. Benjamin Braun's philosophy of learning math—redefining success through failure—needs to be planted in all our math classrooms. If resistance is not encountered, you will never build resilience. You will never actually be doing mathematics. Yet, millions of kids are denied mathematics every day by taking lacklustre excursions holding safety ropes. Nobody is going to fall and get bruised up. Coddling our children with mathematics is an insult to both children and mathematics.

In 2014, Bruce McLachlan, the principal of Swanson School in Auckland, New Zealand, took a huge risk. A risk with dividends he never would have imagined. He junked his "safe" playground for one that had cinder blocks, logs, tall trees, mud, and hidden corners. Kids ran around with sticks as though they were auditioning for *Lord of the Flies*. He wanted kids to tumble, fall—and yes—hurt themselves. He felt children needed to be freed from the "cotton-wool" of 21st-century parenting and educating. The results were beyond even his expectations.

Energy and concentration went up in the classroom; bullying and vandalism went down in the school. And, kids did get hurt—initially. But, after time, understanding the rough terrain and becoming resilient to repeated scuffs and scrapes, even injuries went down. This is exactly what our mathematical playground should be like—adventure with adversity. Then—and *only then*—will our students feel alive and happy with mathematics.

The inert education that Whitehead referred to a century ago was all encompassing—mental and physical exercise that was rewarding because it was rigorous and risky. Four decades of being in and out of the jungle gave me a lifetime of resilience. In fact, I got pretty banged up. And, much like the school in New Zealand, the mathematical injuries of incorrect solutions, misunderstandings, and incomprehension lessened. But more than that, it's the patience and persistence that my brain adopted for learning mathematics—sorry, *yearned* for learning mathematics. Little did I know that resilience was going to be transferable. Mathematical resilience didn't just save my life. It gave birth to what you are holding . . .

After over a year of luck, hard work, and a substantial financial investment, I was ready to open the first math store/school in North America—the Right Angle. We were in a historic village just north of Toronto. The building was right beside a very popular confectionary that made mouth-watering chocolates and ice cream.

There was a partnership with Queen's University to send two student teachers to do their practicum here. The Museum of Mathematics in New York City was going to be involved with the merchandising in the store. Ed Burger, a mathematician and president of Southwestern University, was going to pay a visit in 2016.

Never in my wildest dreams could I have imagined opening such a "happy" place to learn and teach mathematics. I never could have imagined being at the summit of everything I wanted so quickly. I was at the top all right—the top of a roller coaster. As incredible as it is to think about, this wasn't my destination—the rapid descent that followed was.

The week before we were about to open, there was a fire. The first fire ever in this historic building that was built in the same year as the Chicago Fire—1871. The whole building suffered smoke damage. My dream of opening a "Math Exploratorium," a place that offered supposed redemption and salvation of my teaching career, literally went up in flames.

Along with the dream was the loss of borrowed money and loss of a road map of my life after quitting teaching. I was at zero; while at the bottom of one journey, I was at the paradoxical peak of another. I was at *shunya*. I was at nirvana. I was home.

One morning of August 2014, I remember sitting on the edge of my bed realizing that I had lost everything. I had been a single father for a few years now. The bed that I was sitting on was in my old bedroom back at my parents' house. Penniless at 50. Almost sounds like the title of a tragic novel. I worried about how I was going to support my kids and their mother. I worried about how I was going to rebuild a career so relatively late in life. I was frustrated. I was anxious. I was worried.

What I was not was . . . unhappy. I strangely waited for a perhaps predictable, immobilizing sadness to seep into my life. It didn't. I had lost everything that I could possibly imagine. Retelling the story to people, their reaction of shock and grief was stronger than mine—that's because I didn't have one. Where was it? Why wasn't it revealing itself? Why was I still so unreasonably happy?

Trying to curate something as ambitious as the Right Angle involved going beyond having a keen interest in math. It necessitated harnessing all the available energy and passion to seek out everything magical and magnificent—books, puzzles, games, and mostly, outstanding math educators. Even picking out the colors for the walls and the furniture needed to reflect the social, experiential, visual, auditory, and tactile learning environment that children long for in mathematics.

Almost every available math book was bought for the lounge area. Today these books are in my office, constant reminders of a dream that seems distant—often to the point of nonexistence. But, it was built. And, in one day in March 2014, it was gone. It was meant to be gone. Failure and loss could never have been so perfectly orchestrated—by agents and forces that are completely unfamiliar to me.

We lose money and time, yet we still have extraordinary obligations to meet. Sometimes you have to resuscitate your life. But, a volatile cleansing of physical assets can allow you to see clearly the value that mathematics has in your life and the impact that it can have in coping with devastation. (If I was teetering at the apex of Maslow's Hierarchy of Needs, satisfied with a great teaching career, a home, maybe a cottage and vacations, writing a book on the happiness of mathematics would be challenging to construct.)

Writing a book on the happiness of mathematics needed blindsiding by the erasure of hope. The fire was a midwife to the next chapter in my life. It was the most blessed set of *misfortune* I could have ever had hoped for. The love of mathematics needed a vacuum to assess the enormity of this uncharted adoration with clarity and conviction. Happiness. It's unveiling could only be so pronounced in a condition of such loss. The resilience that came with playing with life's numerical grass blades for hours upon end was indeed transferable.

Doing hard math problems with learned patience and persistence is not only a portal to appreciate and understand the true currency of mathematics, but the tiny stockpiling of mental resilience maybe gives us a subconscious strength to endure. It most certainly gives us a conscious appreciation of our most immersive moments—those tiny shards of detailed joy that need only be communicated back to us. The beauty of life, replete with all its swirling emotions, is a fractal—repeating itself over and over, infinitely, into the smallest details of experience and wonder.

I would never wish what happened to me on anybody—yet I would never have seen mathematics so clearly without landing in an abyss. Getting back out, reporting on seeing only white light and not darkness, was a function of embedded resilience. The happiness of math. It does exist. It is independent of competency and fluency in the subject. It is far more dependent on struggle and failure—the most valuable human commodities for learning and gratitude. As such, it is for everyone. More important, so is its hopefully now unveiled happiness.

Alas, happiness would be nothing without laughter and the funny moments that make up our lives. Mathematics can make us laugh. Sometimes we are laughing *with it* and sometimes we are laughing *at it*. It's time now to transition from the sweet sadness to the sweet madness!

CHAPTER 9

Thirty-Seven

Laughter

Arithmetic is being able to count up to twenty without taking off your shoes.

—Mickey Mouse

The innocence of children is perhaps captured no better than when they taste new food for the first time. Graces, manners, and customs are hilariously absent when a baby rejects the offerings from a frustrated parent in no uncertain terms. At this time, children's faces are portraits of pain and obstinacy that borders on cartoon exaggeration.

The communication is unrefined, but it is highly effective. The crying, screaming, and stiff-arming not only keep the evil root vegetable at bay, it should make you rethink your approach to giving the nourishment and flavor that children deserve.

For most of us, math was the *orange guck* of education. And, schools worldwide have been serving this historically unsatisfying gruel for over 50 years. The packaging might have changed (fancier textbooks and fancier calculators), but the content and the approach have yet to see a revolution of any significance. Most people still hate math!

Finding medians of triangles might have been crucial to people during the baby boom—a mathematical procedure having all the drama of a cheese sandwich—but today it only qualifies as the pogo stick of mathematics. The uncontested Canon of mathematics still must be learned by *all* of us. Correction—*endured* by all of us. We are still solving math problems involving digging ditches, rowing boats upstream, heights of kites, angles of kites, and of course, how old Mary will be in seven years.

A MATHEMATICIAN'S LAMENT

Poor Mary. The fascination with her age and that of her brothers, sisters, cousins, and friends is where whatever intrinsic interest children had for mathematics was traded in for a fresh batch of societal disdain. Mary was supposed to help kids understand algebra. All that Mary did was help kids hate algebra—to see it as an intrusive tool to decode age riddles for the purposes of finding out things that Mary should really know. Kids should have only known Mary through her lamb.

Now she is also known as a buzz killer for algebra.

Generation after generation of good intentions of serving up the math equivalent of cafeteria fish sticks with fancier plates not only created generation after generation of math-haters, it launched an avalanche of Pinterest photos, memes, YouTube videos, and Facebook groups all climbing over each other to denounce, spoof, and ridicule the 500-hour total incarceration they endured with mathematics in school.

When as mentioned before—and still not enough—that 30 percent of the population is committed to cleaning toilets over doing a math problem, referring to imprisonment regarding math is within the radius of reality. The reality is that kids should be tasting the delicious offerings of mathematics every day, not resigned to processed staples that have been around for half a century.

Unbeknownst to the surly and sarcastic young adults who have turned math hatred into a cottage industry of T-shirts and mugs to proudly display math anger, phobia, and illiteracy, a mathematician—of all people—beat them to this ranting summit. You might have heard of him, Paul Lockhart—only the most quoted person in this book. Lockhart took the hill of math education and chose to die on it. But, he didn't perish. With a combination of deep understanding of mathematics and writing chops/style of a pissed-off Anthony Bourdain, Lockhart absolutely demolished the rickety structure of pseudo-mathematics. *A Mathematician's Lament: How School*

Cheats Us Out of Our Most Fascinating and Imaginative Art Form created its own lore.

There is very little known about Lockhart (and only one YouTube video). There is only one documented interview from 2009. It's short, but it is so *Lockhart*! Below is an excerpt from that interview:

> We all went through this awful math experience. Then people grow up, have a kid or two, and now they suddenly believe in it and want their kids to have this same miserable math education? I don't get it. "This was boring and awful in eighth grade, and it has not been useful to me as a successful adult, but I really want my child to do it." I would understand it more if parents were storming the barricades in protest! People who admit no math ability feel that their opinion about math instruction is valid. That is mystifying. I can't dance, but I know that, so I don't give any dancing advice.

The "Lament" has become a cult hit in the mathematical underground. It has given a voice to a rebellion that is now subconsciously steering the math revolution. The book takes no prisoners and offers zero apologies. The absence of diplomacy is important to note. It signaled a situation that mathematics was not being displayed with the poetry and imagination that encompasses its true nature. Lockhart not only championed the heart and humanity of mathematics, but he also went absolutely medieval on those who were damaging the soul of mathematics.

Lockhart more than validated the frustration of teaching inconsequential mathematics in an assembly line–like fashion and fervor. The mechanization of teaching—which lamentably includes efficient and expedient math instruction—has been heavily criticized by one of the most important voices in education, Sir Ken Robinson:

> Teaching is a creative profession; not a delivery system.

Mathematics was never going to have the best fate in schools. The soil was missing that key nutrient: *creativity*. The mathematics that is showcased in schools is a reflection of this neutered state. Hierarchal unpacking of mathematics, standardized tests, inert knowledge, disingenuous applications, disconnections, disinformation, and dystopia: these are the sour fruits left when all the life is sucked out of mathematics.

If it can drive a teacher to quit . . . just imagine what it does to our general population that gets subjected to this false and soul-crushing image of math. A collective sublimation of anger results in a world where math exists only for comedic pleasure. It's time to visit this postapocalyptic society of funny math alienation.

The first stop must be the most circulated *someecard* about the failure of understanding math. *Someecards* were created in 2007 to satirize the maudlin sentiments of Hallmark cards. They have over five million likes on Facebook and even an android app now. They are omnipresent in social media feeds. A quick Google image search of "math and *someecards*" will lead you to some of the darkest humor about society's reflections on math. In this collection of stinging satire, the standout must be this one:

> How I see math word problems: If you have 4 pencils and I have 7 apples, how many pancakes will fit on the roof? Purple, because aliens don't wear hats.

Humor can only work if it is within arm's reach of reality—anyone's reality. Unfortunately, the reality that creates sentiments involving putting math problems and nouns in a blender is a sizeable one. However, not all who file mathematics under "sarcastic analysis" are people who struggled with understanding math. Lockhart's essay (and then book) was wildly circulated in the math community because his viewpoints were peppered with sarcasm and humor. He kept grinding that pepper mill over the blandest offerings he saw in math education. To this day, I have never laughed so hard, throwing the back of my hand against the pages of comedic gold with confident proclamations of . . . "yes!"

Lockhart not only validated the claims of the self-relegated underclass of mathematics, he unknowingly became kind of a Spartacus hero to them—not to save math education, but save them *from* math education. From mathematicians holding PhDs to YouTube stars like Vi Hart to flunking students, the world of math comicality is filled with a motley crew of commentators and contributors. If there could be a mythical bar that could house these folks, it would be something like the cantina found in the pirate city of Mos Esley in *Star Wars*. Lockhart would be Han Solo.

> I don't see how it is doing society any good by having its members walk around with vague memories of algebraic formulas and geometric diagrams and clear memories of hating them!

> —Paul Lockhart

THE FUNNY NUMBERS

But, even before getting to the land of mathematical absurdity that still exists in some schools—two words: long division—we can find plenty of levity in numbers. The number 42 is synonymous with Douglas Adams's *The Hitchhiker's Guide to the Galaxy*, specifically it being the answer to literally everything. After seven million years of ponderous calculations, the supercomputer Deep Thought figured out "42" was the answer. A larger supercomputer named Earth was built to figure out what the hell the question was in the first place. This cult piece of fiction has now embedded 42 as having no other importance. So, in some way, art in this case *influenced* life.

Numbers have the propensity for being funny when used in exaggeration. How cold is it outside today? Funny answer: minus 3000 degrees. What makes the answer especially funny is that the number is unrealistic and smashes through the barrier of both Celsius and Fahrenheit measurements of Absolute Zero (–273 and –459). Citing a very large number for a hot summer's day is funny all right, but knowing that parts of the sun can experience temperatures in the millions tempers the intended jocularity with the reality of physics.

Naturally, we use small numbers to indicate sarcastic popularity of something—"according to a recent survey it was found that seven people do not like chocolate in North America." The number used in the best-selling book *Catch-22* was simply the result of a brainstorming session to see what number was funnier than the rest. For some inexplicable reason, Joseph Heller and his agent, Robert Gottlieb, just settled on the subjective chuckling factor of "22." And now, even if one has not read the book, *Catch-22* is deeply entrenched when describing paradoxical situations in life.

There are other numbers we chuckle at for a variety of reasons—the last number in the 60s is almost a rite of passage for teenagers to giggle at in the throes of their adolescence. But, the number that seems to have the longest history of merging in our pop culture through films must be . . . (*drumroll, please*) . . . 37! Don't laugh. Well, laugh and keep laughing, but don't laugh as to the perceived randomness of this choice. It's not mine. It's the tongue-in-cheek research of writer/comedian Ed Brawley from Brooklyn. Here are some of his references:

- A peasant in *Monty Python and the Holy Grail* jokes about how he died at 37.
- The universe is 37 hours long in *Men in Black*.
- Bill Murray's chest is only 37 inches in *Stripes*.
- There have been 37 members in *Spinal Tap*.
- *My Cousin Vinny* starts with the line "This one is 37 cents."

There are other references Brawley cites, but the greatest reinforcement of his claim of 37 being the number that invokes the most chuckling is when he delves into the mathematical characterization of this number. Accompanied with some basic number theory about odd and prime numbers, Brawley sketches a funny portrait of why 37 could be so funny:

Odd numbers are funnier than even numbers. Even numbers are not funny because they look like they have their shit together, like even if they get split up in half, there are still two numbers there that can keep each other company. As if somehow they are more happy and confident because there are two of them, like stray dogs that found each other or the Winklevoss twins. It's not funny when someone has their shit together. Odd numbers are less stable, more off-kilter and wacky. They are like a guy with a tie all loose sweating and trying to carry too many papers and the papers are going everywhere. Now that is funny. Thirty-seven is also a prime number. Prime numbers are like odd numbers' odd number. They are so weird you cannot divide them by anything. Prime numbers are like those Andy Kaufman comedians.

Brawley goes into more detail about the size of 37 as a prime number that is something along the lines of *Goldilocks and the Three Bears*— not too big and not too small. While his main intention is to provide a lighthearted examination of 37 being so darn funny, he does take the readers through a decent hike through prime numbers and their almost stubbornness to be divided by anything. And while he ends his article with confidence and definitiveness about 37 being amazingly funny, his very next sentence—his last sentence—is a rebuke of all this official stamping of 37 as being the leader in laughs, saying "the search continues." Yes, it does . . .

BASE 10 FRUSTRATION

In Alex Bellos's *The Grapes of Math: How Life Reflects Numbers and Numbers Reflect Life*, there is a survey in which 30,000 people were asked what their favorite number was. (Full disclosure: I'm not sure about my favorite number, but I can tell you that my *least* favorite number is 10!) Thankfully, the number 10 had a position ranking of the 23rd most favorite number. Ha! It couldn't even crack the top 20. You know why? The author gives us a simple but scathing explanation—"it is always prostituting itself as the number for approximation."

But base 10 numbers are also accomplices in shady misinformation at times. For example, do you notice that the probability of rain in a weather forecast is always a multiple of 10—40 percent, 60 percent, 70 percent, etc.? Why is that? Surely, the meteorological conditions are not conspiring to ensure that the chance of precipitation always lands on a chunky multiple of 10, right? Right.

What is happening here is that due to weather forecasters being the bane of many people's disdain in terms of prognostication—"they never get the weather right"—actual statistical analysis of previous conditions usually spits out not-so-comfortable numbers.

While a number like 70 percent could come out, more than likely it is something like 67 percent. But that number is accompanied by a statistical error that usually allows it to extend to these "safety" base 10 numbers. The weather people are already under assault. Reporting the precipitation with a number like 67 percent is going to only increase the barbs hurled toward the weather folks. And, buttressing this number with analysis and statistical error isn't going to help matters.

Remember, we are quite often dealing with a hostile crowd in terms of math endearment. And yet, sigh, a labeling of "72 percent" on a bar of fine chocolate for its cocoa content is taken at face value. Crazy world. When 70 probably means 72 in the weather world and 72 means 70 in the confectionary world.

Understanding statistics is paramount in understanding so many different branches of knowledge in society. If everyone had a basic knowledge of, let's say, standard deviation, there might be less hype, panic, and distortion of numbers by the media. Ironically, in one of the most important parts of a democratic society—voting—the most care is taken there to reflect what polling numbers mean. So, if a candidate has 43 percent of the vote, there is often some qualification about the margin of error—usually 3 percent, which means the candidate's real popularity could lie between 40 and 46 percent.

But, what is often missing in a television explanation of the error is the confidence interval—which is usually around 95 percent. What this number tells us is that 19 out of 20 times, that candidate's poll numbers will sit between 40 and 46 percent. But, 1 in 20 times—I hate to break it to you— we (the statisticians) could have completely whiffed on our analysis and these numbers are all wrong! Exhibit A: 2016 US Presidential Elections.

Math illiteracy, phobia, and dislike don't just drive themselves off a cliff when school is finished. We know that because of the tomatoes constantly chucked at math in social media. But, when these folks—the *loud minority*—are not penning witty rejoinders to painful math experiences, they are employed in a variety of professions that must use mathematics in responsible ways. While the intentions are good, the results are often not so.

PERCENTAGE MISUSE

The go-to culprit in fanning the flames of reader/viewer fascination is the use of percentages. Oh no, they are being used correctly, but they are almost always reported without any context. Let me give you an example.

Let's say a research has found that drinking beer gives men a 50 percent greater chance of getting a certain type of cancer. Imagine the shock that finding would stir among people. However, I would calmly still be drinking beer because nobody has conveyed what the actual incidence of that cancer is! What if it's 1 in 10,000 males, or 0.01 percent? A 50 percent increase now means that the incidence is now 1.5 in 10,000 males. You see how deceiving percentage changes are without the whole story? That is why media loves percentages. They tell a teeny-weeny bit of truth and boost story lines. Telling more truth would severely temper the attention-grabbing potential of "naked" percentages.

Inasmuch as math is funny in the outside world, where it is sadly and ironically the absolute goofiest is inside the classroom—ground zero for math comedy. Social media, comedians, T-shirts, mugs, and such would have no material to work with if mathematics didn't partner up with education eons ago. And, guess who had a ringside seat to this circus for almost 20 years? Most people run away to the circus, I ran *away* from one. It only saved my entire life.

Grade 4. It was the first time I was in a portable. As a kid, I loved it. It felt like I was in some kind of cabin at camp. Growing those bean plants inside that reeked mightily would not be the smelliest thing we would do that year. That would be long division. *Really*? you might wonder. *Aren't you exaggerating a little bit here*? Well, not really. We were working with numbers in the thousands. Yes, but so what?

Dividing something like 4,280 by 64 is standard fare. The problem was that we were dividing 64 by 4,280! Really! What in blazes would a nine-year-old kid be taking away by employing long division with such a ridiculous divisor? Oh wait . . . I have 64 slices of pizza and 4,280 friends coming over. How much pizza does everyone get?! I'll tell ya . . . a chunk of crust, a nibble of mozzarella, and a sniff of pepperoni!

If long division even gave a hint as to what was going on, it might have a leg to stand on. It doesn't. It's a completely cloaked algorithm that has the excitement of a cheese sandwich. Just use a bleepin' calculator! Save some time to work on the next unexplained piece of mathematics. Long division. It should be called "Wrong division."

Being relatively good at math made me somewhat impervious to the banality that seeped into other students. However, I was keenly aware that most of the mathematics that I was doing was procedural and computational. Subconsciously, I think I was looking to go outside the boundaries of problems—find ways to use what little math knowledge had been accrued to hack into the status quo of doing things. That is one of the minor gifts of knowing mathematics. To be able to see the world through another lens—to see perspectives, dimensions, and texture that are undetectable without such an aid. As a student, my greatest moment of mathematical subversion came in grade 8.

Mr. Zichowski, or Mr. "Z" as he wanted to be called by his students, was right out of *The Wonder Years*. Funny, irreverent, and helluva fun math teacher. At some point during the year, he announced that there would be a math contest. I always loved the idea of a math contest. Not that it was a contest so much, but that the questions had the potential to be different than the pedestrian ones offered for homework and tests.

Mr. Z said that we would be given 30 questions to work on. The twist was that our score would be calculated by "correct responses divided by total time to finish." He told us each question was worth 1 point. I reasoned that if I did one question quickly and got it correct, my ratio score would be unbeatable. I was right. Not only did I finish first, but a rule was put in the following year that all questions must be attempted. I christened this rule, the "Singh Rule." To this day, that is still one of my proudest math moments—far more satisfying than any A on a calculus test.

Trigonometry has a bizarre standing in our society. It is seen, in North America at least, as some minor peak of mathematics achievement. It also carries some kind of lore due to its false idea of impenetrability by students. In the 1983 movie *Risky Business*, Miles, the friend of Joel (played by Tom Cruise) utters this funny line in the movie—"I don't believe this! I've got a trig midterm tomorrow, and I'm being chased by Guido the killer pimp." There is a crazy car chase and potential life endangerment, and only a mythical topic like trigonometry can be woven into the scene and not feel like a supporting player.

Trigonometry, while often hated, is mythologized to such a ridiculous point that it enters the script of an iconic 1980s film. Meanwhile, for me, it represented the nadir of high school mathematics—zero intuition about its relationships and bucket loads of application questions that made teaching them an embarrassing experience.

SOHCAHTOA. The older sibling of "FOIL" and the cousin of "CAST." This was the low point of teaching mathematics—mainly, because it wasn't mathematics that was being taught, but supposedly clever mnemonics to act as a full-time understudy for *understanding*. As such, trigonometry is poorly understood, and static diagrams and equations offer nothing in terms of an intuitive insight of the relationship between triangle measure, the unit circle, and trig functions.

Trigonometry needs movement—circular movement. It needs to be shown as a film, not as portraits in a museum. Reducing sin, cos, and tan as compartmentalized ideas to be memorized as opposed to interwoven concepts to be understood yields misunderstanding and mystification of its true identity (*ha ha . . . pardon the unintentional trig joke*).

Punch in the sin of 61 degrees on a calculator. The answer will be 0.8746 . . . However, what most students fail to realize what that decimal answer really means. First of all, let's convert it to a more comfortable format of percentages. Our answer is now 87.46 percent. But, what is this percentage describing? Remember, the sine ratio in a right triangle compares the "opposite" side to the "hypotenuse." So, every time you have a triangle that is 61 degrees, the length of the opposite side will always be 87.46 percent of the hypotenuse. Always.

In fact, teachers should not let kids use a calculator or trig table. They should want students to use common sense/estimation to figure out trig ratios and angles. Teachers could even turn it into a game. "Who can tell me what the tan of 17 degrees is?" Students might eye that angle and draw a triangle like the one below (figure 9.1).

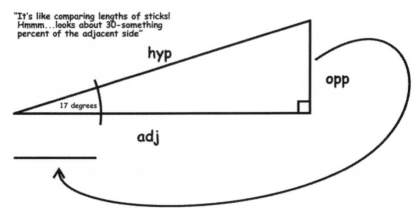

Figure 9.1.   The anatomy of basic trigonometry.

They might use their fingers or a paper's edge—no rulers allowed—and estimate what percentage the short opposite side is compared to the longer adjacent side. Any answers less than 50 percent would be applauded. Those above 50 percent could be asked about getting their eyes checked for glasses. Not too surprisingly, a few kids would be able to get close to the answer of 0.305 or roughly 31 percent.

Kids still hated trigonometry, but they at least comprehended their misery. Unfortunately, when it came to the applications of trigonometry, the teachers are of little use—except for being extremely sympathetic toward growing annoyance at the irrelevance and idiocy of math problems.

THE MISERY OF KITES AND HIKES

Flying kites. Hiking. Boating. Sports. These are fun things. You know what ruins the fun? Trigonometry. Like loud, uninvited guests showing up at a party without food or wine, sin, cos, and tan show up in every single hobby, event, or occurrence in which you can draw a triangle. And since you can throw three coins in the air and have them fall with almost 100 percent probability that they won't form a straight line—

trigonometry has become an intrusive and pompous ass in so many of life's pleasurable activities.

Nobody in the history of the planet has flown a kite and wondered about its height or angle of elevation. Nobody. Not even the lip-biting authors that write these dopey problems. You are flying a kite. It's above the ground. Nothing more to see here, folks. But wait, here comes trigonometry. Did you measure off how much string you have on your *moving* hypotenuse? Because I am sure it's going to be brought up, especially if sin or cos starts grilling you . . .

Do you like hiking? The better question is, do you want to keep liking hiking? For if you do, never ever go on a hike with the kids who pack measuring tapes, clinometers, and calculators. Now, since these questions are trumpeted as applications of trigonometry—*Math Teacher Lie #1: You Will Use Trig in Everyday Life*—it is kind of fair game to analyze these situations of casual math interference for their logic.

Often two people go for a hike. It's fair to assume some kind of friendship exists. Yet, somehow, they get separated—*want to* get separated—by some specific distance. Alicia and Bob are 84 feet apart. Did they have a fight? What is the purpose of going on a hike together if you are not going to walk together? The only purpose would be to construct a ridiculously contrived storyboard about finding the height of an approaching cliff (figure 9.2).

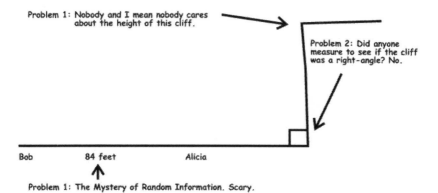

Figure 9.2.   *The trigonometry application that is fake news.*

Most people are not concerned about any cliff heights, but they might be interested in how Alicia and Bob knew they were 84 feet apart. What happened right before they discovered this information—sort of like the mystery of the prior microseconds of the *Big Bang*? When they came to stop—probably because they realized how dumb it was to walk apart—how did they measure off 84 feet? Not so much with what did they use, but how did they do it . . . *why* did they do it? Did they hire some anonymous third-party guide to carry out these grunt tasks? Jason Wilkes wrote a great book called *Burn Math Class: Reinvent Math Class for Yourself* in 2016. Pretty sure the trigonometry sections in high school textbooks caught the flames first—if not, they should have. It gets worse.

One of the common verbs found in trig questions is *notice*. Yolanda notices that the angle to the top of the roof is 41 degrees. Azir notices that the boats are 120 feet apart. Notice? Do we really notice things that need at least a few minutes of calculation? Are these folks armed with glancing powers of acute measurement? If so, then *the aliens have indeed landed.* We notice things like mustard on our shirts and cloudy days. The only time we even attempt to quantify our observations with a casual looksee is when we are commenting on the crowded nature of some event—"Sally noticed that the workshop called *Making Trigonometry Fun for Students* was poorly attended."

Recently, in a new textbook to boot, I saw a question about the angle of declination from a sleeping koala bear to a eucalyptus leaf. Yessiree, sleeping animals were now being cruelly employed in trigonometry. The guess here is that the hike takers and kite flyers had quit.

All those trig questions. Remove the contrived storyboards for a minute. No kites, planes, buildings, flagpoles, boats, and such. Just label the triangles with letters of the alphabet. Now, is this question still captivating? Yes. Carry on. No, wait. Throw it in the garbage.

The problem is that the mathematics classroom should never have been given the ammunition of such mocking. Lockhart wrote a whole book on the disaster that is math education—the *Big Bang* of honest, uncensored, and jubilatory exorcism of inane and insane mathematics. Everything said and written since—in books, social media posts, TED Talks, and YouTube videos—is a result or a reflection of one of the most needed commentaries in the history of math education.

By concentrating on what, and leaving out why, mathematics is reduced to an empty shell. The art is not in the "truth" but in the explanation, the argument. It is the argument itself which gives the truth its context, and determines what is really being said and meant. Mathematics is the art of explanation. If you deny students the opportunity to engage in this activity—to pose their own problems, make their own conjectures and discoveries, to be wrong, to be creatively frustrated, to have an inspiration, and to cobble together their own explanations and proofs—you deny them mathematics itself. So no, I'm not complaining about the presence of facts and formulas in our mathematics classes, I'm complaining about the lack of mathematics in our mathematics classes.

—Paul Lockhart

Math education sometimes, unintentionally, acts like a hot dog, composed symbolically of almost cartoonish filler that Lisa Simpson once horribly imagined—pigeons, raccoons, rats, and boots. Unfortunately, when you spend millions of dollars on standardized tests that have their questions harvested from mathematics that is substandard, diversionary, painfully anachronistic, and steered blindly by political agendas, you get what you paid for—seething, accrued hate from every walk of life.

If mathematics was simply *this*—and nothing more—the pain would be somewhat tolerable. But, to know what mathematics *really is* and how unimaginably distant it is from what gets taught in school and conveyed in the media is a frustrating gulf to bridge. It's almost impossible to build. But ways must be found . . . soon.

Where would you start? How could you possibly convey that the historical unhappiness with math that millions have experienced is the incorrect fate and that the one that *awaits* so many of them—happiness—is the truthful and magical one? The Jason Wilkeses of the world have gotten it partially right—torch mathematical ideas that seem dull, boring, and diversionary. And yes, recreate your own understanding of mathematics. But, do so through a filter of human interest and curiosity. Be serious, but allow yourself to laugh at the misfiring and miscalculation of math's relevance.

We might be imperfect. Math might be perfect. But we are perfect in pointing out the times and places where math's intervention is quite imperfect. Mathematics is everywhere. Inasmuch as that seems like a blessing, it is also a curse.

We must count our blessings and do the occasional face-palms when mathematics throws the lampshade on its head at 2 a.m.—with nobody in the room. Pointing out that an ice cream cone is made up of a cone and half a sphere is one thing. Asking a math question about the volume of ice cream using formulas involving π is quite another. It turns a captive audience into a captured audience. Capture equals defeat. Defeat leads to boredom. Boredom + social media? Do the math . . .

They say it's all fun and games until someone loses an eye. In the case of mathematics, it's all fun and games until someone *closes* their eye. Laughing at and with math is a lighthearted way of dealing with our painful disconnection from mathematics. In the end, that is what we all are looking for—to be connected. Mathematics never disconnected from us; we disconnected from mathematics. We just should ensure that the outlets we use lead us—lead us *back to*—the original story.

If laughter was to serve only one purpose in mathematics, it should be to warn us that whatever we have experienced was an imposter for math. The real McCoy? It's about leisurely wandering and wondering. It's about finding all the mental, physical, emotional, and spiritual connections to patterning and symmetry. To find purpose . . .

CHAPTER 10

Phi

Connection

There is a spirituality to mathematics that few people understand.

—David Krumholtz ("Charlie" from *NUMB3RS*)

When Carl Sagan departed this planet for the heavens that he waxed poetic almost his entire life for, we not only lost a great scientist, we lost a passionate advocate for exploring the universe. And, while his exploration involved planets, stars, galaxies, quasars, and black holes, it was quite often framed in an unapologetic romanticism. He made us believe that the universe was an intimate space with intrinsic marvel. He made millions of people connect to his *billions and billions* of stars.

When he died, it felt that we got unplugged from our own universe. We had lost connection. The core of Sagan's philosophy was an almost religious devotion to disproving our lonely existence in the cosmos. His interest about extraterrestrial life went well beyond just finding it—he wanted to communicate with it. His fascination for humanity's ultimate prize—to turn science fiction into just science—was highlighted in his best-selling book, *Contact*. In 1997, just one year after his passing, Warner Bros. released the feature film *Contact*, starring Jodie Foster and Matthew McConaughey.

It's hardly a surprise that the alien civilization that contacts Earth uses mathematics to pierce through the din of cosmological noise— the pulsations that are heard are in prime number sequence from 1 to 101. (Sagan for some unknown reason included 1 as a prime number). No astrophysical event could generate such a fundamental and foundational pattern. That scene in the movie is one of the most gripping scenes of the entire film—to have that silence broken by mathematics.

THE COSMOS TAKES AND GIVES

When Sagan died, there was a large void left behind. We had lost our ambassador for the endless night sky. Too often, people like Carl Sagan are once-in-a-lifetime occurrences. They create and set a bar so high for teaching and storytelling that they become iconic social personalities that get referenced for many generations. It would have been more than okay to have lived in a time where there was only one *Sagan*. It would turn out—insert *Yoda* voice now—that there would be *another*.

What's that saying? "A brother from another mother." The very year that Sagan died, a young thirty-something astrophysicist and cosmologist named Neil deGrasse Tyson became Frederick P. Rose director of the Hayden Planetarium of the Rose Center for Earth and Space. The world did not know it (maybe the universe did), but the mantle had been passed.

While Sagan's voice had a charming twang that was gentle yet authoritative, Tyson's baritone voice is compelling yet gentle. The result is the same—to infect the general population with hope and wonder about the stars above. In 2014, the inevitable happened. The 1980 TV show *Cosmos: A Personal Voyage*, which introduced millions into joyful scientific inquiry, got a sexy reboot with Tyson carrying on the legacy of Sagan.

While the *Cosmos: A Spacetime Odyssey* debut hit a total of 8.5 million viewers across all the television stations that carried it, the maturing power of YouTube made Neil deGrasse Tyson—already a rising social media star—a household name two years earlier in 2012. At that time, he was interviewed by *Time* magazine and was asked this question: *"What is the most astounding fact that you can share with us about the universe?"* A YouTube video was made that year summing up that interview, replete with powerful sounds and visuals. It is inspirational. It is emotional.

"When I look up at the night sky and I know that yes, we are a part of this universe, we are in this universe, but perhaps more important than both of those facts is that the universe is in us," Tyson said. "When I reflect on that fact, I look up, many people feel small cause they're small and the universe is big, but I feel big because my atoms came from those stars. There's a level of connectivity. That's what you want in life. You want to feel connected."

There it is. The central message of that video is about human connection—to see, touch, and feel together. The universe, as large as it is—and in the video Tyson wants us to feel *big* not small on this tiny blue dot—has its spiritual locus in simple awareness of our life's events. Many of these events are microscopic and, yet, they are the constant reminders that the universe is abundant in gifts. The most prominent ones are woven inextricably in sacred patterns in life—literally. The splendor envisioned in Kafka's world will always be found in the microfibers of mathematics.

Add the two numbers. Sounds like such a vague and innocent command. A benign third number is generated. Add the front two numbers in this seemingly disconnected trio. A fourth number now pops into existence. Add the front two numbers . . . *again, and again, and again* . . . The endless repetition of a simple addition prompt is what gives something like a sunflower its dizzying array of seeds. The Fibonacci Sequence that is displayed in this dense packing of spirals is now relatively well known due to a healthy introduction in middle school.

$$1, 1, 2, 3, 5, 8, 13, 21, 34, 55, 89, 144, 233, 377, \ldots$$

What is not as well known is that the terminating ratio of 1.61—phi—that is found by dividing any number by the previous number is not unique to the 13th-century man who bred rabbits. Oddly enough, if you start with any two seed numbers and the rule about adding the front two numbers, you will always get phenomenal phi in the end. Throwing, for example, any two birthdays in your family and employing what seems like a hardly binding operation of addition of consecutive numbers always results in a "speed limit" of division that is 1.618—a common representation of this irrational number.

Such a simple sequence, its engine being the addition of two *freshly baked* numbers. The mathematical consequence resulting in a terminating ratio of a number being slightly bigger than one-and-a-half. And yet, this aptly anointed *golden* ratio is sculpted into our bodies, reflected in our architecture, and resourced by design technology. In nature, most of us are now familiar with this ratio in things like sunflowers, pinecones, and nautilus shells. Just search for images of the golden ratio and this is what you will most likely get.

From Euclid's mention of the golden ratio in 300 BC, the number—also known as the Golden Number, Golden Proportion, Golden Mean, Golden Section, Divine Proportion, and Divine Section—has only grown in mystery and intrigue. The book *The DaVinci Code* by Dan Brown only accelerated that idea. We literally started looking for this almost spiritual number everywhere.

But, even that began to have some push back as articles began to crop up in 2015 trying to debunk the importance of these ratios in design. Naturally, this only brought out debunkers of this debunking. And, so a mini flame war began on the Internet with the soldiers from the math army volleying back some rather sulfurous remarks. On the website www.thegoldennumber.net, they were listed in an almost badge of honor: "*appalling, sensationalist, dangerous, stupid, underinformed nonsense, an exercise in ignorance and conceit, seething with misinformation, misleading, utter nonsense, profound ignorance, lame, entirely incorrect, click bait, what a troll, simplistic, naive, puerile, opinionated, unsophisticated, boring, fallacious, etc.*"

In a hardly surprising move, the website that posted the article (Fast CoDesign.com) by John Brownlee titled "The Golden Ratio: Design's Biggest Myth—The Golden Ratio Is Total Nonsense in Design: Here's Why," took down all the comments. It turns out that the collective anger of the math community was not only bang on, but up to date. The new Aston Martin has 16 specific instances of the golden ratio all over its design. Aston Martin's website says the following:

> Every inch of DB9's form is designed for elegance and balance. The simple beauty of nature guides the design of DB9, with the "golden ratio" setting all proportions. The result is a profile where every line, dimension and proportion works in harmony. Combine this with the near perfect weight distribution, provided by a lower engine placement, and you have a DB9 balanced on sight and in experience.

SEARCHING FOR GOLD

When you start arguing against mathematics, you are basically saying that you could be from the Flat Earth Society. Sure, not every instance of the ratio of two measurements resulting in 1.61 will mean something, but donning a cynical hat isn't seeing things with eyes wide open. It's seeing them through off-putting squinting ones. Wide open eyes usually are optimistic and happy. Squinting ones can be pessimistic and sad. Don't be sad.

One full cycle of the DNA's double helix yields a length of 34 angstroms and a width of 21 angstroms—numbers found in the Fibonacci Sequence. The spiral of galaxies—specifically the arms of these spirals—also have the golden ratio embedded in their formation. From our own microscopic building blocks of life to the heavenly bodies of our galaxies, the number 1.618—a smidgen more than "one-and-a-half"—is most certainly divine. It's in our creation. What more we can extract from this is left up to one's faith. When it comes to mathematics, that faith should be eternal.

The chapter you are reading is the only one in the book where I suffered a bout of writer's block. One might think that the momentum of writing the previous chapters with the breezy gift of *flow* would carry on in crafting the penultimate chapter—especially one that binds all the other ones. The stoppage was not due to lack of energy or creative emptiness. It was, ironically—but, after a few weeks of deep reflection, not surprising—in the throes of witnessing one of the most emotionally connecting moments of my entire life.

On August 20, 2016, my country—Canada—came to a full stop. Canadian readers will not need reminding of what transcending, once-in-a-lifetime event occurred on that date. But, for those of you living in various parts of the globe, it is crucial that I *attempt*—there's that word again—to parlay that event into what mathematical connection can act like and inspire to be.

The Tragically Hip is a Canadian band that has been around for 30 years. That is not what is important. The Tragically Hip play a style of music that is a mixture of bar room blues and folk-rock musings. That is not what is important. The Rolling Stones kind of borrow from the same chest of influences with a British twist of things. They have been around for over half a century. So, at this point, there is nothing terribly special about some band called the Tragically Hip.

It's only when you focus on the lead singer/songwriter does even a band like the Rolling Stones fall by the wayside. In all honesty, most bands would. The lead singer of the band is Gord Downie. In early 2016, Downie was diagnosed with terminal brain cancer. He and his band made it a mission to do one more cross-country tour to celebrate the very essence of their longevity—Canada.

To be specific, Downie canvassed our country's short history and geography—subjects that are often equally as unpopular as math—and wrote songs about remote towns, prison stories, unremarkable lakes, longitudinal lines, famous athletes, and explorers. All of which could easily occur in the country you live in. These stories are universal.

What Downie did was connect them to us in a way that they got permanently imprinted in our psyche and identity. We discovered ourselves through a country that we thought we knew. He voiced a scrapbook of memories and events that were once disconnected—discarded even—and gave them to a whole country, a gift to be cherished forever.

The resonance was truly measured for the first time that late summer Saturday night. Our national television station, CBC, broadcasted the whole concert across the country. People watched in bars, backyard parties, hockey arenas (of course), parks, and streets. To describe what the event was is not important. To describe that tears flowed from coast to coast is. Three decades of deep connection to the most subtle and human parts of Canadian existence could only elicit such a response—especially knowing that the giver of this was living courageously and magnanimously through an accelerated winter of his life, which explains why I got derailed from writing this chapter on connection. I was consumed with how the poetry of music, when channeled through warmth and honesty, can leave you with such an emotional and lasting investment. A fellow Canadian musician and author, Dave Bidini, offered up this deeply binding state with the following: "It was torturous in a lot of ways because of the emotion. Hard to see it through the tears, right? But also, grateful that I was seeing it that way, that my heart was so invested in it."

> Likewise, I am grateful for trying to connect the brilliant deposits of mathematics—its people, its history, its random discoveries, and its remote understanding—with an unapologetic love. I am eternally thankful to see math through a prism of such emotional investment.
>
> To be inspired by an artist like Gord Downie and weave a story that is uniquely my experience, but, with uninhibited thoughts and emotions, makes that story about mathematics not just universal—but universally happy. Hopefully, it has been confirmed by this point, but there is still some more work to do in viewing math as a human connection that is deep and everlasting. Viewing math is one thing; viewing it slowly is quite another.

SLOW DOWN AND SMELL THE SUNFLOWERS

Most of us don't live in a slow society. We all know that. Unfortunately, we have lived in it long enough for people to research the detrimental aspects of hyperactivity—that most of us at least know about if not intersect daily—and write compelling books on the topic.

Carl Honoré wrote a book called *In Praise of Slow: How a Worldwide Movement Is Challenging the Cult of Speed.* That book came out in 2004. This is in the domain of the negative environment that math education has been nested in for at least 20 years. It has not been impervious to the consequences of this cult. Au contraire.

Ask any teacher and they will tell you how overwhelmed they are by trying to cover as much curriculum as possible in the time that they have. Since nobody has yet invented a clock of more than 24 hours, having more and more topics to cover has only resulted in shrinking time frames to teach mathematics—and boy oh boy, we use the word *teach* liberally here.

Hurrying the learning of mathematics is a death sentence for learning mathematics. Sorry, there is no point in candy-coating the effect of a hyperkinetic tour through the land of mathematics. Paul Lockhart didn't do it over a decade ago, so I won't do it here. The exploration and deep learning of mathematics, like any art form, takes time—time to be creative, reflective, and mentally productive. The classrooms of our students need to allow quiet time to unplug and relax.

Others inspire us, information feeds us, practice improves our performance, but we need quiet time to figure things out, to emerge with new discoveries, to unearth original answers.

—Dr. Ester Buchholz

We have seen positive results of *Slow Movement* in eating, exercise, sex, and work. Not on that list is *learning and appreciating mathematics*. Perhaps Mr. Honoré will consider this inclusion in a future edition of his book! The sad reality is that no earnest or meaningful adoption of being slower in digesting mathematics has taken place. Chronic indigestion and bloating is still being reported by thousands of students, with many full-grown adults still belching up chunks of trigonometry to this day. (*As you can see, the effects of the previous chapter are still lingering*).

Based upon its release date of 2004, the suggestion of when Carl Honoré must have been hatching his idea for a book on slowing down must have been near the end of the 20th century. This coincides with the early generation of Internet users. With little surprise, a book that dove deeply into the effects of surfing the web and screen time was released: *The Shallows: What the Internet Is Doing to Our Brains*.

If Carl Honoré has been passionately telling all of us to put the brakes on so many parts of our lives, then Nicholas Carr has identified one of the side effects of trying to be the *Roadrunner*. Subtracting his obsessive-compulsive disorder in trying to capture this ground-bird without motive, *Wile E.* was a good influence in taking his time scheming and inventing creative machines!

A declining amount of time—quite often our own fault—and an overreliance on the connectivity of the Internet has started to impact the neuronal wiring of the brain according to Carr. Essentially, he says, we have become *skimmers* to manage and process all the information we think we need—the key word being *think*. The group that this is adversely affecting the most is young children, whose screen time goes often unmonitored. So, what do you think might be happening to learning math if the time devoted to thinking is decreasing along with the physiological ability to process its deeper and richer connections? Anxious and confused children with self-esteem and confidence in jeopardy.

The learning of mathematics can be a joyous and happy experience if given space and time. Reducing these variables in a world already compressed and stressed will shade this kind of learning into obscurity. All of us—educators and parents—need to reclaim the learning environment of our children and fashion it in a way that allows for them to move slowly and leisurely through the sunny fields of mathematics.

We will be successful if we can just do that. But how? The key is to combine the simple ideas of arithmetic with intrinsic motivation and curiosity—without the feeling there is a stopwatch around. Kids and teachers should treat arithmetic as a necessary trail to journey on. But, the pacing should be more like a Sunday hike—not a Monday cross-country run. A slower pace allows for gazing, foraging, and resting. Beyond giving the proper conditions for meaning and purpose in learning mathematics, it makes the trek a happy one.

The connections to mathematics don't have to be many, but they should be deep, creating strong roots of understanding. We are capable—just don't rush us. If you do, we won't understand. And even those who might catch a glimpse of the interconnectedness of math, our desire to stay and *poke around* will be undermined by the unnecessary need to simply move on.

One area that has shown the greatest traction for the *Slow Movement* is how we eat and how we talk about food in the technologically overrun parts of the world. We are not only being instructed to spend more time eating, we are also encouraged to speak about the details of food—where it is grown, how it is harvested, and such. Some of the most successful restaurants are the ones that emphasize this farm-to-chef-to-table narrative. Every step is important. Every detail has potential beauty for discussion.

Just listen to chefs like Thomas Keller of the French Laundry or Dan Barber of Stone Hill at Blue Barns speak about food. They speak about it eloquently, passionately, and, above all, *slowly*. Math classrooms need to be like this. Children need to discuss their understanding and misunderstanding with each other in ways that affirm their interests. As Dan Meyer said a few years back, math should serve the conversation—not the conversation serving math. This needs to happen for authentic and natural mathematical learning to occur. If not, speed and correctness will continue to be false idols in math education. Children need time and space—literally—to understand and appreciate math.

ZOOMING IN AND OUT FOR CONNECTION

Look at the connecting power of a number like phi. If we can find magic and meaning in the smallest details and have conversations about them, we have a better chance of bonding with mathematics. Luckily, phi is not the only constant than can evoke wonder. There are many more. A number like e—2.718—while outside the scope of this book, has its own book (*e: The Story of a Number*). Unfortunately, only a small segment of the population intersects with it as it is traditionally encountered and discussed in calculus courses. However, millions around the world were exposed to this number in 2004.

On August 19, 2004, Google announced its share price of $85 in its IPO. Incidentally, that stock has only grown by well over *1,000* percent since then. However, what got buried in this major announcement and was overlooked by almost everyone was the size of this IPO. Most media outlets reported it to be 2.7 billion. Some even had the word *strange* written in the headlines.

What few were reporting was that the actual number was $2,718,281,828—the number e times one billion. The fine folks at Google were paying homage to a number they obviously had affinity for. It's a remarkable number that pops up in topics like probability, statistics, and calculus.

While phi and e are kind of the all-stars of numbers, their similarity and difference yields even a deeper journey into the mathematical universe. They are both irrational in that they cannot be expressed as a fraction, but unlike phi, e is transcendental. This simply means that it will never be an answer of an algebraic equation with rational coefficients. In fact, there are more of these kinds of "snobby" transcendental numbers than the algebraic ones.

There are two types of connections that are needed in life—the macro and the micro. They differ in size, but not in their magnitude of relevance and impact. The universe, well, that easily takes care of finding connection in something large. It's as large as it gets. What about the teeny-weeny stuff? The grass blade—a reoccurring symbol in this book—has both poetic and mathematical significance. The bar for pondering was raised—or since we are talking about the minutiae of life, perhaps *lowered*—by this simple structure of nature.

The only direction left to go is smaller. Nothing could be smaller than a number in math, each one telling a story. Quite often these stories become surprisingly expansive in their charm—opening like beautiful flowers in time-lapse videos. We need to tell these stories, some of these being lost treasures of mathematical discovery. Storytelling is not only the best way to teach, it is the best way to connect—to share that space between the two of us. One more story to tell. We have come full circle . . . literally.

CHAPTER 11

Pi

Hope

Far away are my highest aspirations. I may not reach them, but I can look up and see their beauty, believe in them, and try to follow them where they lead.

—Louise May Alcott

Every year on March 14, notifications of Pi Day rain down on social media. The most common posts have the iconic symbol—π—playfully merging with an actual pie with some joyous message announcing this whimsical date. While the extent of the celebrations might be limited to baking and tossing pies with some light reflections about this gold medal of constants, the fact that it is recognized by a chunk of the globe is the more important milestone. Even the United States House of Representatives supported the designation of Pi Day back in 2009.

However, due to the variance of formatting the date, specifically the order in which to write the day and month, Pi Day cannot be celebrated in South America, Northern Africa, India, Australia, and large parts of Europe. March 14 is written as 14/3. To complicate matters some more, there are some keen math folks who wish it wasn't celebrated at all. These people would rather hope that the true circle constant—circumference divided by radius (6.28)—gets any celebratory attention. I am not as zealous in these matters, but I am quite sympathetic to Tau Day due to the elegance of working with this *late June* constant (since 6.28 translates to June 28).

TAU VS. π

The mathematical maverick leading the crusade of all things Tau is Michael Hartl. His website, The Tau Manifesto, leaves no ambiguity as to where he stands on the circle constant that needs reverence. Even YouTube math star Vi Hart has created a cheeky and slightly snarky video titled *Pi Is (Still) Wrong*. The Massachusetts Institute of Technology has tried to amusingly mediate this potential flame war by sending out its acceptance letters over the Internet on March 14 . . . 6:28 p.m.

Inasmuch as mathematical and aesthetic appeal Tau might have— and it has lots—there is no getting around the fact that π's lore in our society is quite immense. Even Givenchy had some marketing/branding understanding of the irrational and transcendental power of π and created a men's fragrance in 1998, giving math *even more* romantic notions.

The first person to investigate π seriously was Archimedes of Syracuse—Sophie Germain's mathematical hero/inspiration. Despite not having a calculator or understanding of decimals, Archimedes used the idea of a polygon with an increasing number of sides—showing more "circleish" character—and some crafty trigonometry to get a value for π to 99.9 percent accuracy. After getting to a 96-sided polygon by working through the quagmire of ugly fractions, Archimedes painstakingly mined out the following diamond of results:

$$3\frac{10}{71} < \pi < 3\frac{1}{7}$$

Roughly 700 years later, Zu Chongzhi would *call* Archimedes's method and *raise* him to the point of working with a polygon with 24,576 sides! His value of the ratio of the circumference to the diameter eclipsed the 22/7 standard—355/113 was his result. How good was it? A better approximation wasn't achieved for about oh, another 1,000 years!

And, soon as decimals were fully employed, the almost obsessive goal to extend π to more and more and more decimal places began. And, it hasn't stopped. From getting π to a few hundred decimal places by the end of the 20th century—already well beyond what is even needed in pure mathematics—to now over 13 trillion, the fascination with this circle constant remains as infinite as its irrational structure. It's like a micro-exploration of a boundless universe. We know that it goes on forever. We just want to keep finding more and more *stars*.

Carl Sagan went to the depth of mathematical creativity and optimism, installing his own hope of perhaps a spiritual meaning for the universe, by writing in a dramatic ending to his book *Contact*. Far, far off in the expansion of π—nearing sextillion digits—the digits, when calculated in base 11, showcase their randomness now in nothing but 1s and 0s. The length at which this occurs has its own delightful secret, as it is the product of two prime numbers. The book ends with Ellie Arroway plotting these digits as pixels on a computer screen—revealing an actual circle! A book about an almost universal hope to contact other sentient beings ends with π. So does this one . . .

SOCIAL MEDIA SAVES MATHEMATICS

In many ways, it is not just happiness from mathematics that has been veiled from the public—mathematics itself has been in a collective darkness to most of society. Think about it: until the early part of this century, where was the intersection for the public to explore and investigate mathematics? School.

Very few of us were witnessing the *painful beauty* of mathematics. And, nowhere to be found was any contradicting evidence of the heap of mathematical rubble that every child was laboring through—for the entire duration of their childhood. Yes, Paul, we all got cheated out of *our most fascinating art form*, but redemption à la Shawshank was never in the cards. Breaking out would not lead to any accessible oasis for most. That would all change forever with the technological Big Bang—the birth of social media.

Between the years of 2004 and 2006, Facebook, YouTube, and Twitter were launched. How we connected and communicated shifted to a radical transparency, allowing for an evolving equity among people in sharing information. We all wanted our 15 minutes—and then some—with more permanent soapboxes. The Wild West of creating and disseminating information was here to stay. One of the biggest beneficiaries of this tsunami of web-based communication was mathematics.

If we think of mathematics as a television set, then around this time it went from a post–World War II black-and-white RCA to 4K resolution with OLED technology on a 65-inch curved screen. The revolution was not subtle and . . . it was *televised*.

All the smoldering truth about mathematics being an art form, ripe with gripping history and imaginative heroes, came to life like mythical unicorns. No longer primarily confined to static and limiting textbooks, the often cold and dry mathematical explanations herein were thrown into this social media hopper and finally gave mathematics *back* its color. Mathematics went from cod liver oil in the classrooms to Skittles and Starburst on the Internet.

Facebook, Twitter, and YouTube are now densely populated with dynamic and creative groups and channels that showcase discussions and videos detailing the past, present, and future of mathematics and math education. All the math revolutionaries are here. All the exhibitions are here. All the vibrant discussions are *here*. Why? Because that is where we all are in some form or another.

Neil deGrasse Tyson is not only an accomplished science educator, he is also one of the biggest fans of Pi Day. Already a master of using social media to illuminate and nurture heady ideas about math and physics—aiding in the accessibility and attractiveness of historically uninviting branches of knowledge—Tyson has used his crossover success into pop culture to resurrect some of the most gorgeous ideas involving π.

Thanks to the brilliantly acted 2015 film *The Man Who Knew Infinity*, more of the world now knows of the genius that is Srinivasa Ramanujan. His remarkable ascent into the pantheon of mathematicians from the most isolating and impoverished of conditions—rural village in 19th-century India—has finally settled in as one of the most important stories in this history of mathematics. Self-taught, his obsession and religious devotion to numbers—through poverty, loneliness in England, and finally sickness—speaks to the highest romanticism that we should have for mathematics.

One of the greatest contributions Ramanujan made to mathematics was to *tame* π. While the rest of the mathematical world was obsessed with exploring its irrational tendency deeper and deeper into mind-boggling decimal places, Ramanujan sought to extract and express the hidden symmetries in a number that behaved wildly. Today, thanks to people like Tyson, the surprising patterning and staircase aesthetic of continued fractions that Ramanujan miraculously extracted from π is now the stuff of mainstream fascination (figure 11.1).

$$\pi = 3 + \cfrac{1}{6 + \cfrac{9}{6 + \cfrac{25}{6 + \cfrac{49}{6 + \cfrac{81}{6 + \cfrac{121}{6 + \ddots}}}}}}$$

Figure 11.1.   Ramanujan: The pi whisperer.

THE EMANCIPATION OF MATH

Honestly, you don't even need to know what is going on here to see how the most famous number of irrational behavior seems to now be the result of some mathematical boot camp—sixes obediently initiate each endless scaffold with squares of odd integers. It just looks so damn pleasing to the eye, perhaps even inviting deeper contemplation of what bridge of intuition and intelligence gave the world this gift of magical patterning. Where did Ramanujan really find his inspiration? Was it in the realm of our comprehension or in something outside the radius of logic and talent? It seems fitting that Ramanujan be the last mathematician referenced in this book.

A movie, long overdue, was finally made about him. His mathematical exploits continue to shake heads of the brightest thinkers today. His foray into this sacred realm of knowledge was fraught with almost made-for-television obstacles. And yet, he probably reached the highest summit as to what symbolizes the essence of math—love and devotion. This is where we need to *start* our journey.

Mathematics was developed and discovered by people who were a motley crew of personalities who thought deeply and passionately about the universe of numbers. They were all astronauts, adventurous in their thinking and fearless in their travels. Some were philosophers. Some were court jesters. Some were the apotheosis of sober thoughts. Some were poster children for all things crazy.

Mathematics was handcuffed for the longest time because conservatism—the archenemy of mathematics—was how it was viewed and discussed inside schools. It obediently colored inside the lines with an HB pencil. That is until social media threw it a backpack filled with Sharpies and Crayolas. There is a beautiful Waterboys song called "This Is the Sea." In the song, river means constraint and the sea means freedom. *Math, once you were tethered, now you are free.*

Mathematics now has numerous platforms to strut all its peacock feathers, whether it wants to be scholarly, subversive, or silly. And that is just it. It's not just that mathematics is everywhere in our society as an external expression, its domain of curiosity stretches in every imaginable direction regardless of who you are and where you are. Mathematics will find you.

This entire book has been a long overdue love letter back to mathematics. The inclusion of over 100 pop culture references has been subconsciously purposeful. Mathematics, for me, has never been a checklist item in a list of interests or hobbies. It's never been sitting on some bookshelf as some encyclopedia of knowledge. It's never been about being a subset of life to be clearly represented in some tidy Venn diagram. It has never been something to be corralled and caged. It certainly cannot be described without the use of the most florid language—Faulkner's "kill your darlings" be damned!

Mathematics joyously spills out like a pallet of colors, staining every crevice of our lives, through its intertwining, intersecting, and tangential powers. It does this not despite being mathematical, but because it *is* mathematical. It is not an appendage of human expression; it is its bloody circulatory and nervous systems! The limits of our imagination and the boundlessness of our emotions is where you will find mathematics. Unapologetic romanticism of this hope is the only flag that mathematics needs to fly. And the mathematical endeavor that is raising this flag to its highest peak yet is the Global Math Project.

Launching officially at the Museum of Mathematics in early fall 2017, the Global Math Project hopes to enthrall one million people around the world in its inaugural year with a piece of joyous mathematics called *Exploding Dots*—a mind-blowing experience, created by Dr. James Tanton, that uses the concrete idea of dots and some basic arithmetic sense to propel people from simple binary expressions to calculus! (www.theglobalmathproject.org.)

Something as ambitious—and audacious (a common refrain from James Tanton)—is a by-product of this new digital age of deepening connection. The true colors are now fully visible to everyone. The paradigm shift for mathematics toward unabashed joy and happiness has now been given a proper coronation—uniting the globe through the beauty of math. This new road will not only reshape how mathematics is viewed and explored, but it may lead to an international curriculum—that is rooted in the 21st-century call for stronger number sense, connection, and questioning.

> Nothing is more powerful than an idea whose time has come.
>
> —Victor Hugo

There is much mysticism and magic in π. It's not tethered strictly to the geometry of a circle. It also pops up often in number theory and statistics. It even describes the "windiness" of rivers. If you take the ratio of an actual river's length and divide by its straight, source-to-mouth length, you will get a number. The straightest rivers will have a value close to 1, while those that take a drunken stroll might have values above 5 or so. It turns out that the average meandering ratio of all rivers is about . . . 3.14.

It was intentional for this book to start at Zero and end at Pi. It was unintentional for them to be linked by a circle—one being a *circularesque* shape and the other being the most popular reference for this symbolism-rich shape. While there are literally hundreds of significant meanings of the circle around the world, the one that captures the essence of mathematics—and this book—is the idea that the circle represents the infinite nature of energy in the universe. Hope is eternal. It may seem irrational at times to cling to it, but it does transcend everything that is most human about us. This is where you go "I see what you did there, Singh."

DISCOVERING HAPPINESS NEEDED TIME AND STRUGGLE

This book took 10 years to write. A shortfall of ideas or energy was not the reason for this protracted writing. No. There had to be time inside *and* outside the classroom during the rebirth of mathematics in this golden age of social media. There also had to be failure and loss. This was the cocktail I needed to sip while gazing out at the world, mooning that someday the whole world will see mathematics through gentler eyes.

The evolution of mathematics for the longest time was occurring in the vacuum of academia and education. The intention was noble, but the gravitas that was pinned on mathematics was only pinning it down. Unexplained rationale for preserving methodologies and ideologies for math's preferred state of being institutionalized remained.

Ten years ago, there was little illumination of math's colorful landscape. There was no Museum of Math in New York City. There is one today. There were no social media exaltations of math's beauty. There are literally thousands today. Mathematics in the 21st century has been reawakened to its true majesty. Education now must quickly shift and adapt.

It *must* rethink the value of assessment. It *must* reimagine what classrooms look like. It *must* reconstruct its curriculum to house more number theory, game theory, and graph theory in elementary grades. It *must* reexamine the importance of time. Above all, the mandate for learning and teaching mathematics *must* be governed by the joy and happiness of mathematics—emphatically and unapologetically.

At the risk of everything, we must hoist our sails and go in this direction. Our obligations are beyond practical measures now. They have become morally compelling. Mathematics is being returned to the

world in the only way that has mattered to its historical permanence—
happiness. We are here. We are home.

Life is either a daring adventure or nothing.

—Helen Keller

Strange. Well, maybe not. But I feel like I am back at chapter 1, *zero*.
There is a literal end that needs to be entertained here, but the broader,
philosophical end does not exist—the *limit* of our hopes *DNE*! Swish!
A philosophical bend on a calculus staple at the buzzer.

There is a wonderful pang that I am feeling nearing the inevitable
end. It is one of feeling that there is much, much more to say. Hopefully this book has felt like a conversation on *your porch*. The sun is
coming up. It's this book's *Before Sunrise*. There is one more pop reference left. As I said earlier, all the other ones have just subconsciously
popped out with a desire to make the book a breezy and buoyant read.
The only one that was purposefully sculpted into this book is the one
that is left in front of us. It involves two people. It involves closure. It
is drenched in warmth and joy.

There are too many coincidences in my life to simply keep saying
the word *coincidence*. How is it possible that the best ending I feel that
I can have for this book can come from one of my top five favorite
films of all time, *Almost Famous*. Specifically, its final scene.

In the last scene of the 2000 movie *Almost Famous*, teenage protagonist
William Miller finally gets his interview with musician Russell Hammond, who pays him a surprise visit in his bedroom. William, armed
with his tape recorder and probably a slew of questions, opens with
something simple but profound: "So Russell, what do you love about
music?" There is a noticeable sigh by William just before he clicks his
microphone on, almost indicating—and hinting—that the answer that
he receives will be thoroughly satisfying. Before Russell responds, the
acoustic melancholy of Led Zeppelin's "Tangerine" washes over the
scene. There is exactly a 10-second delay before his response:

To begin with . . . everything.

If I were Russell Hammond, I would have given the exact same answer if the word *mathematics* replaced the word *music* in William's question. It not only sums up my feelings about mathematics, but it has a nice tinge of surpassing infinity when we love something so much.

Mathematics. Wonderfully imperfect humans crafted and discovered this perfect body of knowledge, and I, this thankfully flawed author, made *his attempt* at communicating the magic that lies in that adventurous journey. That magic drifted through almost every imaginable nook and cranny of cultural references, metaphors, and life experiences. Meandering strolls, whimsical diversions, and wholehearted explorations were the result.

And it all came to purposeful rest in a terminating scene in a Hollywood movie that is unassuming and as far removed from the world of mathematics it could possibly be. And yet that scene captures the enormity of mathematics—as the scene does with an equally powerful force, music—with the grace, awe, and reflection that is unsurpassable. In other words, it's damn perfect.

The best moments of all our lives are not only nonquantifiable, they are often ineffable. There are several passages from this book that house unexplored tributaries of thoughts—each terminating, or *not*, at various lengths. While I am resigned to what I was unable to communicate, I am thankful for what I could—that one of life's splendors is mathematics. It no longer waits for us. We have called it out by its right name, from its shadows—happiness.

Index

fatigue, 123
Fermat, Pierre de, 46, 101
Fermat's Enigma (Singh), 10, 46, 48
Fermat's Last Theorem, 46; lore
    of, 47; possible solutions to, 49;
    Wolfskehl and, 48
Feynman, Richard, 61
Fibonacci numbers, 21
Fibonacci Sequence, 151; DNA
    double helix and, 153
The Fifth Estate, 114
55 (number), 21
Flat Earth Society, 153
Flatland (Abbott), 71
The Flintstones, xix
flow, 84–85, 91
*Flow: The Psychology of Optimal
    Experience* (Csikszentmihalyi), 84
Fonda, Henry, 32
Fortnow, Lance, 97
42 (number), 137
Foster, Jodie, 149
fractals, 72, 73; in African societies,
    76; from Collatz Conjecture, 126;
    teaching of, 79
Fractals: A Graphic Guide
    (Lesmoir-Gordon), 76
*Fractals: Form, Chance, and
    Dimension* (Mandelbrot), 75
*Fractals: Hunting the Hidden
    Dimension* (2008), 76
fractions, 5; addition of, 27, 110;
    division of, 24; improper, 24;
    mixed, 24; multiplication of, 110;
    subtraction of, 27
French Laundry, 157
French Revolution, 10
Fresno Pacific University, 13
Friedman, Glen, 44

galaxies, 51
gambling, 102; reckless government
    promotion of, 119
game theory, 119
Gardner, Martin, 86, 95
Gauss, Carl Friedrich, 10; number
    theory and, 18
Gazette (magazine), 13
geometry, 167
Germain, Sophie, 9, 10–11
Givenchy, 162
Global Math Project, 167
"The Golden Ratio: Design's
    Biggest Myth—The Golden Ratio
    Is Total Nonsense in Design:
    Here's Why" (Brownlee), 152
*The Golden Ticket: P, NP, and
    the Search for the Impossible*
    (Fortnow), 97
Goldilocks and the Three Bears, 139
Google, 15, 52; share price of, 158
googol, 52
Gottlieb, Robert, 137
Graham, Ron, 54
Graham's Number, 6, 54, 55
*The Grapes of Math: How Life
    Reflects Numbers and Numbers
    Reflect Life* (Bellos), 139
Greitens, Eric, 7, 121, 122
Grime, James, 83
Ground Zero, 9
Guinness Book of World Records, 54
Guns N' Roses, 127

Les Halles Cookbook (Bourdain),
    43–44
Hallmark cards, 136
handshakes, *22*, 24
Hansel and Gretel (nursery rhyme), 37

Russell, Bertrand, 41–42;
  accomplishments of, 43;
  Wikipedia page on, 44

Sagan, Carl, 31; death of, 150;
  extraterrestrial life interest of, 149;
  mathematical creativity of, 163
Sand, George, 15
sarcasm: sarcastic analysis, 136;
  small numbers to indicate, 137
satire, 136
Sayers, Dorothy, 29
scalar representation, 71
screen time, 156
selling fear, 112
Serling, Rod, 57
set theory, 58, 62
Shakespeare, William, xviii
*The Shallows: What the Internet Is
  Doing to Our Brains* (Carr), 156
shunya, 4
Sideways (2004), xxi
Siefe, Charles, 2
simplicity, 15, 26; underlying truth
  of, 27; of zero, 5
The Simpsons, 52–53, 114; lotteries
  in, 118
sin, 143
Singh, Simon, 10; on Fermat's Last
  Theorem, 46; on Wolfskehl, 48
skimming, 156
Slow Food Movement, 27
Slow Movement, 156, 157
Smashing Pumpkins, 8
social media: boredom and, 147;
  creativity of, 164; number theory
  on, 54; Pi Day on, 161; stars of,
  150
society, 136; slow, 155
Socrates, 1, 8

someecards, 136
Southwestern University, 129
Spartacus (1960), 121
speed of light, 8
spirituality, 4
square roots: of negative numbers,
  69; of positive numbers, 65
squares, 20
"The Star" (Taylor, Jane), 51
stars, 52
Star Trek II: The Wrath of Khan
  (1982), 76
Star Wars (1977), 137
statistics, 140
status quo, 142
Steinmetz, Charles, 71
Stevens, Michael, 53, 62
Stone Hill at Blue Barns, 157
Stripes (1981), 138
"Student Success" workshop, 127
Su, Francis, xx
subtraction, 27
Sudoku, 81–82; proof, 85
suicide, 48
Super Bowl, 108
supercomputers, 137
Swanson School, 128

tan, 143
"Tangerine" (Led Zeppelin), 169
Tanton, James, 167
Tau, 162
Tau Day, 161
Taylor, Jane, 51
Taylor, Richard, 74
teachers, 16; high school, 18;
  quitting, 136
teaching, 70, 88; fractals, 79
TED Talks, 76, 84; *Math Class
  Needs a Makeover*, 87

About the Author

Sunil Singh was a high school math and physics teacher for 19 years. Before he quit teaching in the classroom in 2013, he had taught everything from basic math for junior students to IB math for honors-level students. He has worked in a socioeconomically challenging environment of an inner-city school in Toronto and at the prestigious International School of Lausanne in Switzerland. His vast experience teaching math in every setting imaginable has helped him become a leader in creative math education in North America. Since 2005, he has given over 40 workshops on kindergarten to grade 12 mathematics at various locations—math conferences, faculties of education, and even the Royal Conservatory of Music in Toronto.

In addition to having been a regular contributor to the *New York Times* "Numberplay" section, Singh works full time as a math consultant for Scolab, a digital math resource company in Montreal, Canada. As well, he travels all over North America as a speaker and promoting Family Math Nights in local communities. He is an integral component of the Global Math Project, and his ambassador designation is helping him communicate the beauty and happiness of mathematics throughout the world. He can be reached at (sunilsingh@mathjester.com) and followed on Twitter @Mathgarden.

Made in the USA
Middletown, DE
07 March 2019